Bloomsbury Professional Tax Insight

Cryptocurrency and Bitcoin

GW00685495

Bloomsbury Professional Tax Insight Cryptocurrency and Bitcoin

Ben Symons

Barrister, The 36 Group

Bloomsbury Professional

LONDON · DUBLIN · EDINBURGH · NEW YORK · NEW DELHI · SYDNEY

BLOOMSBURY PROFESSIONAL

Bloomsbury Publishing Plc

41–43 Boltro Road, Haywards Heath, RH16 1BJ, UK

BLOOMSBURY and the Diana logo are trademarks of Bloomsbury Publishing Plc

Copyright © Bloomsbury Professional Ltd 2020

Reprinted 2022

All rights reserved. No part of this publication may be reproduced or transmitted in any form
or by any means, electronic or mechanical, including photocopying, recording, or any information
storage or retrieval system, without prior permission in writing from the publishers.

While every care has been taken to ensure the accuracy of this work, no responsibility
for loss or damage occasioned to any person acting or refraining from action as a result of
any statement in it can be accepted by the authors, editors or publishers.

All UK Government legislation and other public sector information used in the work is Crown Copyright ©.
All House of Lords and House of Commons information used in the work is Parliamentary Copyright ©.
This information is reused under the terms of the Open Government Licence v3.0
(http://www.nationalarchives.gov.uk/doc/open-government-licence/version/3) except where otherwise stated.

All Eur-lex material used in the work is © European Union, http://eur-lex.europa.eu/, 1998–2020.

British Library Cataloguing-in-Publication Data

A catalogue record for this book is available from the British Library.

ISBN: 978 1 52651 261 1

Typeset by Compuscript Ltd, Shannon
Printed and bound by CPI Group (UK) Ltd, Croydon, CR0 4YY

To find out more about our authors and books visit
www.bloomsburyprofessional.com. Here you will find extracts, author information,
details of forthcoming events and the option to sign up for our newsletters

Foreword

One common feature of literature of the apocalypse is that the meaning of what is hidden is hoped to be revealed. Another, is that an angel or other ethereal creature is required to guide us through the complexity of symbols to the clarity of revelation. The guide we seek, like any currency we use, should hold our trust and confidence.

This is a lot to ask of the author of any legal text, particularly when their work is designed for both practitioners and members of the public alike. All the more so, when the publication covers the topics of cryptocurrency and taxation. Readers may embark upon the journey towards understanding these two difficult subjects and their interplay with some trepidation.

All is not lost, however, for Ben Symons has taken on the unworldly task of assembling this handbook. He has produced a short and accessible guide which identifies the key concepts and issues for taxing authorities and taxpayers considering the UK tax treatment of cryptocurrencies, in particular Bitcoin.

The 16 chapters are structured in such way as to navigate a clear path for the informed or uninformed reader: chapters 1–3 define and explain cryptocurrencies; chapters 4–8 explore the taxation consequences for profits, losses and gains depending on whether they are classed as trades, gambling, investment or other miscellaneous income; chapters 9–11 address cryptocurrency 'mining', Airdropped cryptoassets/tokens, forks in the Blockchain and their tax consequences; chapter 12 considers taxes for employees paid in cryptocurrency; chapters 13–14 compare the potential treatment of non-domiciled individuals for inheritance and capital gains taxes; and chapter 15 deals with the VAT consequences of goods and services purchased with cryptocurrency, or if cryptocurrency is used as a form of payment.

As is acknowledged in the conclusion, the scope for the use of cryptocurrency is not yet known, nor is the full extent of the tax consequences carved in stone. Nonetheless this work provides not simply a building block but a secure foundation which can be mined when seeking answers to the full range of enquiries.

Judge Rupert Jones
Judge of the Upper Tribunal
The Rolls Building,
London EC4
11 December 2019

Contents

Chapter 1

Introduction

1.1 Bitcoin[1] is now just over ten years' old.[2] In its early days, Bitcoin was traded largely by cryptocurrency enthusiasts trading amongst themselves. The first recorded transaction in Bitcoin took place on 22 May 2010 when Lazlo Hanyecz paid 10,000 Bitcoins to fellow crypto trading enthusiast, Jeremy Sturdivant, for two Papa John's pizzas.[3] The nominal value of a bitcoin was then around $0.004.

Bitcoin first received widespread publicity in 2013 when the FBI closed down the notorious online drug trafficking syndicate, Silk Road.[4] Syndicate users were paying for drugs with Bitcoin to try and preserve their anonymity.

Then in November 2013, Bitcoin received more positive publicity. A letter by then Federal Reserve Chairman, Ben Bernake, was tabled at a US Senate Committee on Homeland Security and Government Affairs hearing: Beyond Silk Road: Potential Risks, Threats, and Promises of Virtual Currencies. He expressed cautious optimism that virtual currencies potentially 'offered faster, more secure and more efficient payments systems'.[5]

More recently in 2017, there was an explosion in the number of entrepreneurial ventures in both London and Silicon Valley seeking to capitalise on the revolutionary opportunities opened up by Bitcoin's underlying Blockchain technology. The price of a bitcoin soared to nearly $20,000. The 10,000 bitcoins Lazlo Hanyecz paid for two pizzas back in 2010 were worth nearly $20 million by the end of 2017.

---

[1] The term Bitcoin refers to both the software, the network and the actual currency itself. To distinguish the cryptocurrency from the software and the network, it is referred to as 'bitcoin' throughout this publication while the software and the network are referred to as 'Bitcoin'.

[2] Satoshi Nakamoto, the founder of Bitcoin, mined the first 50 bitcoins, known as the genesis block on 3 January 2009.

[3] https://cointelegraph.com/news/a-brief-history-of-bitcoin-10-years-of-highs-and-lows; https://bitcointalk.org/index.php?topic=137.0.

[4] *United States v Ross William Ulbricht*: www.documentcloud.org/documents/801103-172770276-ulbricht-criminal-complaint.html.

[5] Letter from Ben Bernake dated 13 November 2013 to the US Senate Committee on Homeland Security and Government Affairs hearing: Beyond Silk Road: Potential Risks, Threats, and Promises of Virtual Currencies.

Bitcoin has generated enormous amounts of publicity. Most recently, the stratospheric price rise of Bitcoin along with the boom in other cryptoassets has attracted investors who are making both large gains and large losses. This has resulted in both HMRC and taxpayers having to grapple with how cryptocurrency and cryptoasset transactions should be treated from a UK tax point of view. This publication provides an in-depth analysis of almost all the UK tax issues affecting cryptocurrency.

Chapter 2

What are the different types of cryptoassets?

2.1 This publication primarily addresses the tax treatment of cryptocurrencies by reference to Bitcoin.

The Swiss Financial Market Supervisory Authority ('FINMA') states that there is no generally recognised categorisation of cryptoassets either in Switzerland or internationally. FINMA has attempted the following categorisation of cryptoassets based on their economic function:

1   **Payment tokens:** Payment tokens (synonymous with cryptocurrencies) are tokens which are intended to be used, now or in the future, as a means of payment for acquiring goods or services remains of money or value transfer. Cryptocurrencies give rise to no claims on their issuer.

2   **Utility tokens:** Utility tokens are tokens which are intended to provide access digitally to an application or service by means of a blockchain-based infrastructure.

3   **Asset tokens:** Asset tokens represent assets such as a debt or equity claim on the issuer. Asset tokens promise, for example, a share in future company earnings or future capital flows. In terms of their economic function, therefore, these tokens are analogous to equities, bonds or derivatives. Tokens which enable physical assets to be traded on the also fall into this category.[1]

Bitcoin falls into the first category, being a 'payment token'. It is often referred to as a cryptocurrency. It is the tax treatment of transactions involving bitcoins that is the focus of this publication. In some cases, the principles regarding the taxation of bitcoins may be able to be extended to other cryptocurrencies and sometimes, with modification, to transactions involving other cryptoassets. However, this may not always be the case in regard to the tax principles that apply to non-domiciled individuals and VAT. It would be wise to seek advice in these areas.

---

[1] FINMA Guidelines for enquiries regarding the regulatory framework for initial coin offerings ('ICO's), published 16 February 2018.

Chapter 3

What is cryptocurrency and how does it work?

Focus

There is no generally accepted definition of cryptocurrency/virtual currency. However, a cryptocurrency/virtual currency will generally be:

  (i)   a digital representation of value;

  (ii)   that is a general-purpose medium of exchange, but is an alternative to a fiat currency;

  (iii) digital records of which are traded and held over a de-centralised peer-to-peer network;

  (iv) whose digital records are secured by cryptography; and

  (v)   can be converted to legal tender and vice versa.

The distinguishing feature of a cryptocurrency is that it uses Distributed Ledger Technology ('DLT') that in turn uses cryptography to try and safeguard the integrity of its records.

Cryptocurrencies are often described as being decentralised because no central authority, such as a central bank, has regulatory oversight of cryptocurrencies. Fiat currencies are subject to regulatory oversight and are controlled and administered by a central bank.

Cryptocurrencies have no value deemed by law. Their value is determined simply by what someone else is willing to pay for them. Fiat currencies have a value deemed by law.

WHAT IS A CRYPTOCURRENCY?

3.1   The most recent authoritative guidance on describing cryptocurrency comes from the Cryptocurrencies and Blockchain Report dated July 2018 paper of Policy Department A of the European Parliament ('EP Report').

First, the EP Report observes that there is no generally accepted definition of the term cryptocurrency available in the regulatory space.[1]

---

[1] Cryptocurrencies and Blockchain Report by Policy Department A of the European Parliament ('EP Report') July 2018 at p 23 available at: http://www.europarl.europa.eu/RegData/etudes/STUD/2018/619024/IPOL_STU(2018)619024_EN.pdf.

However, after reviewing reports by other central banks, regulatory bodies and supranational bodies, the EP Report provided the following summary of the various definitions of a cryptocurrency:

> 'a digital representation of value that (i) is intended to constitute a peer-to-peer ('P2P') alternative to government-issued legal tender, (ii) is used as a general-purpose medium of exchange (independent of any central bank), (iii) is secured by a mechanism known as cryptography and (iv) can be converted into legal tender and vice versa'.

It is these cryptocurrencies that are the subject of this book.[2]

The key feature of a cryptocurrency, as defined above, that distinguishes it from other forms of electronic currency is that it is not issued by a central bank and it is not deemed by law to be legal tender (ie deemed by law to have a value).[3]

Bitcoin is the most well-known example of a virtual currency, and it was the first cryptocurrency.

However, Bitcoin was not the first virtual currency. The origins of virtual currency can be traced back to the 1990s 'dotcom' boom. E-gold began operating in 1996 and allowed users to open an account denominated in a unit of a precious metal, usually gold,[4] and make payments to one another. On the virtual world Second Life, players transact with one another in Linden dollars (one US dollar equals one Linden dollar).

What distinguishes Bitcoin and other cryptocurrencies from earlier online virtual currencies is:

(1) They are traded and recorded using Distributed Ledger Technology ('DLT'). DLT is essentially a way of recording and maintaining digital ledgers in the form of a digital database, distributed and maintained across a peer-to-peer network of computers or servers, referred to as nodes.

(2) Updating and maintenance of the integrity of the ledger is maintained through the use of cryptography and game theory. It is these features from which the name 'cryptocurrency' is derived.

---

[2] These should be distinguished from central bank cryptocurrencies that are in the nascent phases of being issued BIS Papers No 101 Proceeding with caution – a survey on central bank digital currency By Christian Barontini and Henry Holden, and particularly the diagram The money flower: a taxonomy of money at p 2.

[3] Ibid, at p 2.

[4] Hughes, Sarah Jane; Middlebrook, Stephen T.; and Peterson, Broox W., 'Developments in the Law Concerning Stored-Value Cards and Other Electronic Payments Products' (2007). Articles by Maurer Faculty. Paper 174; see http://www.repository.law.indiana.edu/facpub/174 at 255.

HOW DO CRYPTOCURRENCIES DIFFER FROM TRADITIONAL BANKING?

Traditional banking and building trust

3.2   When doing business, two parties generally need a third-party intermediary to build 'trust' between them so that they can transact. For instance, two parties don't generally inspect each other's financial positions before they do business. They rely on a third-party intermediary, such as a bank, that they 'trust', to verify that each party to the transaction has the money or assets that they claim to have.

In order to build 'trust', a third-party intermediary must maintain the integrity of their ledger systems to prevent inaccurate or downright fraudulent transactions. This is often referred to as preventing the 'double spending problem', ensuring that the same amount of money is not spent twice.

Banks build a reputation as trusted intermediaries by investing in expensive information technology systems and developing sophisticated procedures that maintain the integrity of their ledger systems and ensure their capital adequacy requirements. This trust is further reinforced by having the entire banking system overseen by regulators such as central banks. Customers then transact with reputable banks like HSBC and Barclays based on reputation. They transact on the basis that their counterparty or customer has the money in their account that they say they do, because a reputable third-party intermediary has verified this.

How Bitcoin solves this problem

3.3   The original paper published by Satoshi Nakamoto[5] best summarises how Bitcoin seeks to solve the 'double spending problem' and provide an alternative to traditional banking:

> 'What is needed is an electronic payment system based on cryptographic proof instead of trust, allowing any two willing parties to transact directly with each other without the need for a trusted third party.'[6]

Bitcoin runs on eponymously-named software developed by Satoshi Nakamoto.[7] Through the use of the novel 'blockchain' technology, cryptographic proofs and game theory, Bitcoin seeks to maintain the integrity of transaction records across the network without the need for a trusted third-party intermediary. For this reason, the Bitcoin protocol is sometimes referred to as a 'trustless' system.

---

[5] Satoshi Nakamoto is thought to be a pseudonym for the creator of Bitcoin.
[6] *Bitcoin: A Peer-To-Peer Electronic Cash System* Satoshi Nakamoto, p 1.
[7] Most other cryptocurrencies use a variation of Bitcoin software – Virtual currency schemes- a further analysis, European Central Bank, February 2015, p 32.

A brief history of Bitcoin software and a discussion about how Bitcoin software seeks to achieve a 'trustless' system across the network is provided in further detail below.

HOW ARE BITCOINS ORIGINALLY ACQUIRED?

3.4 To acquire Bitcoins and participate in the Bitcoin network, a participant must acquire a 'digital wallet'. A 'digital wallet' contains a participant's private key that they use to 'sign' and authenticate transactions. Most users acquire a digital wallet when they first install Bitcoin software. For instance, the popular Bitcoin Core software comes with an inbuilt digital wallet. This software also gives them a public address. Both the private key and the public address are crucial to encrypting transaction messages on the Bitcoin network, and therefore to maintain the integrity of the Bitcoin network.

To get started, participants also need to acquire some Bitcoins. There are two ways they generally do this:

(1) Purchase bitcoin with fiat currency. This is usually done through a Bitcoin exchange, like Coinbase. Bitcoin exchanges effectively function as the 'on ramps' to the cryptocurrency world. This is typically how a general member of the public would acquire their first bitcoins.

(2) Act as a 'miner' on the network and get rewarded with Bitcoins by the network for validating transactions.

This software seeks to maintain the integrity of the system by:

(1) First, having a participant who wishes to spend bitcoins broadcast an encrypted message to the network that is digitally signed with their private key. This proves to other participants on the network that:

   (a) it is the participant who is authorising the transaction; and

   (b) the participant holds a valid coin(s).[8]

(2) Secondly, through the use of cryptographic validation by having all nodes on the network agree on a state of the Blockchain. In particular, having all nodes agree on the transactions that have been approved and are to be appended to the Blockchain, and also the order in which these transactions should be appended to the Blockchain.[9] This is achieved by having special 'miner' nodes on the network compete to solve the cryptographic puzzle

---

[8] See particularly Bitcoin and Cryptocurrency Technologies: A comprehensive introduction, Aravind Narayanan, Joseph Bonneau, Edward Felten, Andrew Miller and Steven Goldfeder, p 21. This process also allows other participants on the network to see the number of Bitcoins that the user holds because they know that participants public address.

[9] Bank of England Quarterly Bulletin Q3 262 at 273; Bitcoin: Economics, Technology and Governance, Rainer Bohme, Nicolas Christin, Benjamin Edleman and Tyler Moore, Journal of Economic Perspectives, Vol 29 Number 2, Spring 2015 213 at 217.

created by the participant who wishes to spend bitcoins. This is often referred to as requiring 'miner' nodes to perform a 'proof of work'. Miner nodes have to invest significant amounts of computing power to solve these cryptographic problems. Once solved, 'miner' nodes broadcast their proof to other nodes on the network who can easily verify that the proof is correct. Where greater than 50% of the nodes on the network accept a 'proof of work' as being correct, the transaction is approved, and that block is timestamped and appended to the Blockchain.

Bitcoin seeks to avoid the need for a trusted third-party intermediary.

A BRIEF HISTORY OF BITCOIN SOFTWARE

3.5 Bitcoin started life when Satoshi Nakamoto[10] mined the genesis block over six days starting on 3 January 2009.[11]

Bitcoin was released as open-source software on 9 January 2009, with the first Bitcoin client being hosted at SourceForge.[12]

Bitcoin is open-source software.[13] As such, it can be developed in a public collaborative manner, and anyone can take part in its development.

In the early days, Bitcoin's development was driven by several well-known computer programmers with an interest in cryptography. In particular, the well-known computer programmer Gavin Andresen was primarily responsible for the development, standardisation and promotion of Bitcoin software in its early days. He launched the Bitcoin Foundation in late 2012 with the stated goal to 'standardize, protect and promote the use of Bitcoin cryptographic money for the benefit of users worldwide.'[14]

Wladimir J van der Laan took over the development of Bitcoin software from Gavin Andresen on 9 April 2014.[15] This software is now called Bitcoin Core, and it used by an estimated 80% of users on the Bitcoin network. Bitcoin Core enables users to act as a 'full node' on the network.[16]

---

[10] Satoshi Nakamoto is thought to be a pseudonym for the creator of Bitcoin. Satoshi Nakamoto outlined how Bitcoin worked in his seminal paper *Bitcoin: A Peer-to-Peer Electronic Cash System.*
[11] https://www.investopedia.com/terms/g/genesis-block.asp.
[12] https://en.wikipedia.org/wiki/History_of_bitcoin.
[13] https://bitcoin.org/en/.
[14] https://masterinvestor.co.uk/economics/cryptocurrencies-for-dummies/.
[15] https://en.wikipedia.org/wiki/Bitcoin_Core.
[16] https://bitcoincore.org/en/about/.

WHAT IS THE BLOCKCHAIN?

3.6 The key innovation of Bitcoin is the 'Blockchain'.[17] Blockchain is a particular type of Distributed Ledger Technology ('DLT').[18] Essentially, the Blockchain is a transactional database that is the 'master public ledger'. It records every transaction ever undertaken on the network. It is open for public inspection to anyone who is on the network.[19]

Each time a transaction is undertaken, and a majority of nodes on the network agree that the transaction is valid, a block of data is produced.[20] This block is time-stamped and appended to the existing Blockchain. Similarly, the previous block has been dated and time-stamped.[21] In an identical way, the previous block is chained to the block before it that has been time-stamped, and through this iterative process, a chain of time-stamped blocks stretch all the way back to the genesis block that was originally mined by the founder of Bitcoin, Satoshi Nakamoto, on 3 January 2009. In this way, the blocks of data are said to form a 'Blockchain' that contains the entire history of transactions undertaken on the network.

Identical copies of the Blockchain are collectively distributed, controlled and maintained across computer servers or nodes that form the network.[22] Nodes are essentially people operating Bitcoin client software. Bitcoin is a 'permissionless' network which means anyone can join or leave the network as they please.[23]

Essentially, the Bitcoin Blockchain architecture uses a distributed ledger that creates a de-centralised model in which no central regulator has oversight of the cryptocurrency. The integrity of the ledger is maintained through a two-stage cryptographic process that is discussed further below. This is different from a traditional banking model which is a centralised model. Banks all maintain a ledger with a central bank who oversees the issue of fiat currency and maintains the integrity of the banking system through regulation and supervision of those banks.

As users enter into transactions, the Blockchain needs to be continuously updated for the transactions that they are entering into. However, it is crucial that the integrity of the data is maintained to ensure that a bitcoin is only spent once. The fact that anyone can join the network also creates a serious security issue. It is necessary to maintain the integrity and security of the network against malicious actors who may join the network.

---

[17] Bitcoin wiki: https://en.bitcoin.it/wiki/Block_chain.
[18] EP Report July 2018 at p 15.
[19] Those people generally being nodes on the network.
[20] This is sometimes referred to as the 'hash' of a block because the data that is output if the function of a cryptographic hashing function.
[21] Bitcoin: A Peer-To-Peer Electronic Cash System, Satoshi Nakamoto, p 2.
[22] EP Report July 2018 at p 15.
[23] EP Report July 2018 at p 15.

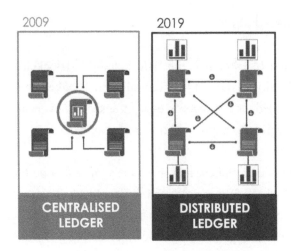

As above, Bitcoin adopts a two-stage verification process to achieve this:

(1) the use of digital signatures/public key cryptography by a participant who wishes to spend bitcoin to prove ownership of the bitcoin's that they propose to transfer and also that the transaction message is genuine;[24] and

(2) a consensus mechanism, known as a 'proof of work', by which all nodes agree on the state of the Blockchain being the transactions that have been approved and the order in which they were approved.[25] In this way, these new blocks can be appended to the Blockchain and provide a complete history of transactions that have occurred.

STAGE 1 – THE PROCESS FOR UPDATING THE BLOCKCHAIN WHEN A PARTICIPANT WANTS TO TRANSFER BITCOINS

3.7 A bitcoin is essentially some form of intangible right. It has no physical existence. A record of how many bitcoins each participant owns is kept in the Blockchain.

Each participant on the network has a 'digital wallet' that contains a private key.[26] This is crucial to the use of 'public key' cryptography that the Bitcoin network uses to authenticate transactions.

Participants have the choice of using a 'hot wallet' or a 'cold wallet'. A 'hot wallet' is a piece of software that allows the participant to store their private key online. A 'cold wallet' on the other hand is a piece of software that stores the user's private key off-line. Bitcoin Core software comes with an inbuilt 'hot digital wallet'.[27]

---

[24] Supra at note 8, p 21.

[25] Bank of England Quarterly Bulletin Q3 262 at 273. Bitcoin: Economics, Technology and Governance, Rainer Bohme, Nicolas Christin, Benjamin Edleman and Tyler Moore, Journal of Economic Perspectives, Vol 29 Number 2, Spring 2015 213 at 217.

[26] A private key is a random string of 51 alphanumerical characters: see Bank of England Quarterly Bulletin 2014 Q3, 262 at 273.

[27] Although there are many other choices of both 'hot wallets' and 'cold wallets'.

The Bitcoin address of each participant on the network acts as their public key. These addresses are widely available and published to all participants on the network.[28]

When a participant on the network wishes to transfer bitcoins, they broadcast two transaction messages to the network. One transaction message is signed with their private key, encrypting that message. The participant also broadcasts a plain unencrypted version of the transaction message to the network. Other nodes on the network can use the participant's public key, a random string of alpha-numeric characters constituting their public address, to decrypt the encrypted transaction message. If both the decrypted transaction message and the plain unencrypted version of the transaction message are the same, which they should be, this proves that the sender of those messages used their 'private key' to sign the transaction.[29] This effectively proves the authenticity of the transaction message.

The other participants can also check how many bitcoins a participant has because they know that user's public address. All relevant bitcoins associated with that address will be contained in the Blockchain.

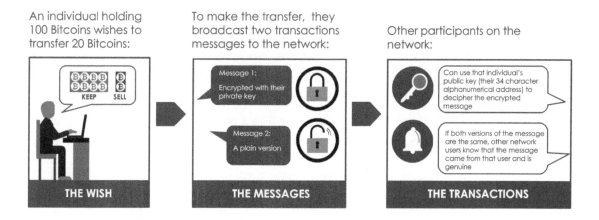

STAGE 2 – THE CONSENSUS MECHANISM

3.8   It is then necessary for all nodes on the network to agree on the state of the Blockchain, and particularly how the Blockchain should be updated to account for the new transaction.

The Bitcoin network is a permissionless network in which nodes are free to join or leave. Typically, there are around 10,000 reachable nodes on the network.[30]

---

[28] A public key / Bitcoin address is a random string of 34 alphanumerical characters, for example: 3n6H2Kp9Bc5W2Ty6Cq25p-0M1Q5Dw8Yu2: see Bank of England Quarterly Bulletin 2014 Q3, 262 at 273.

[29] Bank of England Quarterly Bulletin 2014 Q3, 262 at 273.

[30] https://bitnodes.earn.com/ gives the number of accessible nodes at any particular time.

Computer science has long recognised that there is a problem in trying to get all nodes on a network to agree on a state of affairs, which transactions have been approved and the order in which they were approved. Some nodes on the network may broadcast inaccurate, or even downright fraudulent transaction information to the network. Without safeguards, it is cheap and easy for a node to broadcast an inaccurate or fraudulent message to the network.[31] It is, therefore, necessary to adopt a 'consensus' mechanism to guard against this and protect the integrity of the Blockchain.

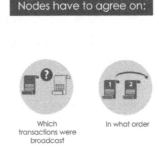

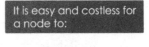

Bitcoin adopts a 'Proof of Work' mechanism by special 'miner' nodes competing to solve complex mathematical problems. Miner nodes have to invest tremendous computational resources in solving these problems. They then broadcast their solution to the network, for other nodes to relatively easily verify and vote on. If greater than 50% of the nodes on the network agree that the 'proof of work' is correct, the proposed transaction is accepted, and the new block is 'hashed', and the Blockchain is updated.

Nodes vote on the "proof of work"

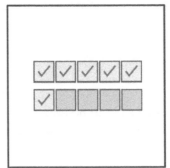

For a transfer to take place, greater than 50% of nodes must approve

---

[31] In computer science, this problem is sometimes referred to as the 'Byzantine Generals problem', named after the seminal 1982 computer science academic paper that came up with the first credible solution to this problem: Leslie Lamport; Robert Shostak.; Marshall Pease. (1982). 'The Byzantine Generals Problem' ACM Transactions on Programming Languages and Systems. Vol 4 No. 3: 387–389.

Bitcoin's 'proof of work' scheme uses the SHA-256 'cryptographic hash function'. The best description for how this 'cryptographic has function' works comes from the Bank of England's 2014 Q3 Quarterly Bulletin:

'The proof of work scheme used by Bitcoin makes use of a special algorithm called a 'cryptographic hash function', which takes any amount of information as an input and creates an output of standard length (the 'hash value'). The function is cryptographic because the hash value produced is different for any change in the input (even of a single character), and it is impossible to know in advance what hash value will be produced for a given input … ….

The Bitcoin protocol requires that miners can buy combined three imports and feed them into a SHA-256 hash function:

- a reference to the previous block;
- details of their candidate block, the proposed transaction or transactions;
- a unique number called the nonce.

if the hash value produced, is below a certain threshold, the proof of work is complete. If it is not, the miner must try again with another value for the nonce. Because there is no way to tell what the value of the nonce when combined with the other two inputs, will produce a satisfactory hash value, miners are simply forced to cycle through nonce values in trial and error …'[32]

The more people that join the network, the easier the complex mathematical problems collectively become to solve by the nodes on the network. Also, over time, more powerful computers and software become available that make it faster to solve these complex mathematical problems. To guard against this and keep it 'costly' for 'miner' nodes to solve these problems, Bitcoin software makes it periodically harder to solve the complex mathematical problems over time, to keep the average verification time at about 10 minutes.[33]

By making it costly for a 'miner' note to solve these complex mathematical problems, it makes it far more difficult and costly for a node to broadcast a message that is inaccurate or even downright fraudulent. It makes it extremely difficult for a group of malicious nodes to attack and 'hijack' the network to broadcast fraudulent transactions. To do this, they would first likely need to command at least 50% of the nodes on the network.[34] Secondly, they would still need to invest tremendous resources trying to solve the complex mathematical problems involved in the 'proof of work' scheme. They would be competing against could 'miner' nodes trying to solve these problems who are already on the network.

---

[32] Bank of England Quarterly Bulletin 2014 Q 3, Vol 54 No. 3 262 at pp 273 and 274.

[33] https://en.bitcoin.it/wiki/Difficulty, the difficulty is in fact adjusted every 2016 blocks. The difficulty is adjusted to keep the average time to solve the mathematical problem constant at around 10 minutes. In theory, the difficulty could either increase or decrease, however with ever greater numbers of 'miners' joining the network, and increasing computer and software power, the difficulty is almost certain to increase. See also: Bitcoin: A Peer-To-Peer Electronic Cash System, Satoshi Nakamoto, p 3.

[34] Bank of England Quarterly Bulletin Q 3, 262 at p 274, however it should be noted that in some scenarios it may be possible to hijack the network by commanding something slightly less than 50% of the nodes on the network.

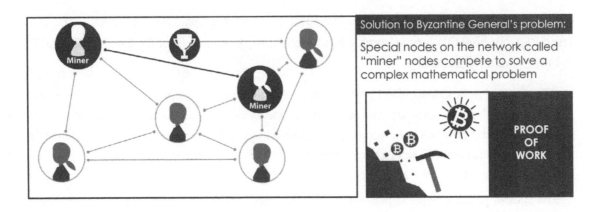

Bitcoin draws on 'game theory' to try and guard against such an attack and maintain the integrity of the Blockchain.

Miners are incentivised to behave honestly by being rewarded with bitcoins for successfully solving a 'proof of work' mathematical puzzle. Miners may also receive a discretionary transaction fee from the participant who wishes to transfer bitcoins.

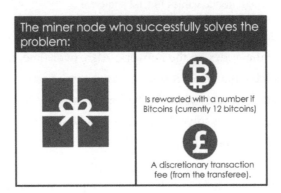

In theory, it is meant to be far more financially rewarding for miners to behave honestly and aspire to be rewarded with bitcoins for solving 'proof of work' puzzles, rather than expending enormous amounts of energy trying to hijack the network and maliciously broadcast fraudulent transactions to the network.[35]

---

[35] Bitcoin: Economics, Technology and Governance, Rainer Bohme, Nicolas Christin, Benjamin Edelman and Tyler Moore, Journal of Economic Perspectives, Volume 29, Number 2, Spring 2015 213 at 219.

Chapter 4

Taxation consequences – cryptocurrency gains – trading, gambling or investment?

ARE CRYPTOCURRENCY PROFITS TRADING PROFITS?

> **Focus**
>
> The taxation consequences of the sale of cryptocurrency are potentially complicated. There is no clear dividing line between whether a profit is a trading gain or an investment gain. Each case turns on its own facts.
>
> The guidance given by HMRC that profits from the purchase and sale of cryptocurrency are generally investment profits subject to capital gains tax is probably true for most individual investors.
>
> However, there may be a small class of investors for whom cryptocurrency profits can be classed as trading profits. This is most likely to apply to hedge funds and a relatively small number of sophisticated individual investors who are 'trading'.
>
> A taxpayer is highly unlikely to be able to maintain an argument that their profits should be tax-free on the basis that they are gambling.

WHAT IS A 'TRADE'?

4.1 Income from a 'trade' is subject to income tax.[1]

'Trade' is defined in *Income Tax Act 2007 ('ITA 2007')*, *s 989* as including 'any venture in the nature of trade'.

---

[1] *ITA 2007, s 3* and *ITTOIA 2005, Pt 2* (trading income).

It was observed in *Eclipse Film Partners No 35 LLP v Revenue and Customs Commissioners*[2] that the Income Tax Acts[3] have never defined 'trade' any further than this. In *Eclipse*, it was observed that the meaning of 'trade' is a matter of law:

> 'Whether or not a particular activity is a trade, within the meaning of the tax legislation, depends on the evaluation of the activity by the tribunal of fact. These propositions can be broken down into the following components. It is a matter of law whether some particular factual characteristic is capable of constituting a trade. Whether or not the particular activity in question constitutes a trade depends upon the evaluation of all the facts relating to it against the background of the applicable legal principles. To that extent the conclusion is one of fact, or, more accurately, it is an inference of facts from the primary facts found by the fact finding tribunal.'[4]

Essentially, whether or not there is a 'trade' is a matter of fact and circumstance in each case. The authorities often refer to the 'badges of trade' that provide an indication one way or the other of whether a trade is being conducted.[5] Sir Terence Etherton C observed in *Eclipse Film Partners No 35 LLP v Revenue and Customs Commissioners*[6] that the list of matters that had been widely regarded as the badges of trade had been helpfully summarised in the judgement of Sir Nicholas Browne-Wilkinson V-C in *Marson v Morton*.[7] Insofar as these matters are relevant to the sale of cryptocurrencies they can be summarised as follows:

- *Is the transaction a one-off transaction or a repetitive transaction?* While a one-off transaction is in law capable of being an adventure in the nature of trade, the lack of repetition may point to it being something else.

- *Is the transaction in some way related to the trade which the taxpayer otherwise carries on?* For example, a one-off purchase of silvery cutlery by a general dealer is much more likely to be a trade transaction than such a purchase by a retired colonel.

- *What is the nature of the subject matter of the transaction?* Was the transaction of a commodity such as toilet paper or whisky that would generally be the subject matter of trade, or was it something related to personal enjoyment.

- *What was the purchaser's intention as to resale at the time of purchase?* An intention to hold the object indefinitely, albeit with an intention to make a capital profit, is a strong pointer towards investment. However, an intention to resell in the short term rather than the long term is some indication against concluding the transaction being by way of investment rather than by way of a deal or trade.

---

[2] [2015] EWCA Civ 95 at [112], [2015] STC 1429 at 1449.
[3] The expression Income Tax Acts collectively refers to *ICTA 1988* and also *ITA 2007*.
[4] *Eclipse Film Partners No 35 LLP v Revenue and Customs Commissioners* [2015] EWCA Civ 95 at [112], [2015] STC 1429 at 1449.
[5] *Marson v Mawson* [1986] STC 463 at 470, [1986] 1 WLR 1343 at 1348 Sir Nicholas Browne-Wilkinson V-C.
[6] [2015] EWCA Civ 95 at [114], [2015] STC 1429 at 1449.
[7] [1986] STC 463 at 470–471, [1986] 1 WLR 1343 at 1348–1349.

Sir Nicholas Browne-Wilson V-C was careful to emphasise that the badges he had listed were not a comprehensive list and that no single badge is in any way decisive of whether there is a trade or not.

IS THERE A 'TRADE'? THE RELEVANCE OF INTENTION OF THE TAXPAYER

4.2   As noted in the last bullet point in **3.1**, the intention of a taxpayer is relevant to whether the taxpayer is 'trading'.

However, it is also interesting to note observations made by other judges on the 'intention' of a taxpayer and its relevance to whether the taxpayer is 'trading'.

The Privy Council in *Iswera v CIR*[8] observed that:

> 'If, in order to get what he wants, the taxpayer has to embark on an adventure which has all the characteristics of trading, his purpose or object alone cannot prevail over what he in fact does. But if his acts are equivocal his purpose or object may be a very material factor when weighing the total effect of all the circumstances.'[9]

Lord Templeman also observed it in *Ensign Tankers (Leasing) Ltd v Stokes (Inspector of Taxes)*:[10]

> 'intention is sometimes[11] illuminated and sometimes obscured the identification of a trading purpose. But in every case actions speak louder than words and the law must be applied to the facts.'

The determination of whether there is a trade is 'impressionistic'.

4.3   As above, it is a question of fact and circumstance in each case as to whether the tribunal of fact[12] considers there is a 'trade' or not. They reach their decision through a weighing of all the different matters, particularly those related to the 'badges of trade'.

Essentially, the tribunal of fact is making an 'impressionistic' judgment as to whether in all the facts and circumstances of a particular case there is a 'trade'. This was the approach endorsed in by Sir Terence Etherton C in *Eclipse:*

> 'It is necessary to stand back and look at the whole picture and, having particular regard to what the taxpayer actually did, ask whether it constituted a trade.'[13]

---

[8] [1965] 1 WLR 663.
[9] *Iswera v CIR* [1965] 1 WLR 663 at 668.
[10] [1982] 1 AC 665.
[11] Ibid at 677.
[12] The first-tier tax tribunal in the case of tax matters.
[13] *Eclipse Film Partners No 35 LLP v Revenue and Customs Commissioners* [2015] EWCA Civ 95 at [111], [2015] STC 1429 at 1449. This approach was also endorsed by Henderson LJ in *Samarkand Film Partnership No 3 the Revenue and Customs Commissioners* [2017] EWCA Civ 77 at [59], [2017] STC 926 at 946.

4.4   The fact finding of the first-tier tax tribunal and their determination of whether there is a 'trade' is crucial.

This is because there are only limited grounds on which the evaluative judgment of the tribunal of fact can be overturned. Essentially, that the tribunal of fact made an error of law, or if the only reasonable conclusion on the facts found is inconsistent with the tribunal's conclusion.[14]

In practice, it is uncommon that a finding by the first-tier tax tribunal that a 'trade' did exist, or did not exist, is overturned on appeal.

JUDGMENTS RELATED TO THE PURCHASE AND SALE OF SHARES

4.5   The purchase and sale of marketable securities is probably the activity that is most closely related to the purchase and sale of cryptocurrency.

It is therefore interesting to consider decisions relating to whether a taxpayer buying and selling marketable securities was considered to be 'trading' for tax purposes.

A review of the relevant case law reveals that there are few guiding principles as to whether a taxpayer is 'trading' in marketable securities. The application of these principles can vary greatly from case to case, and different judges can legitimately arrive at different conclusions as to whether a taxpayer is 'trading'. These cases reinforce that the determination of the tribunal of fact as to whether someone is trading is difficult to challenge on appeal.

The following are a loose set of principles that can be drawn from the cases that consider whether the purchase and sale of marketable securities by a taxpayer can amount to a 'trade':

- The starting point is that generally the purchase and sale of marketable securities is done by way of investment.[15]

- The greater the number and size of purchases and sales of marketable securities, and the more rapid and continuous the turnover of the securities, the more likely this is to indicate that the taxpayer is conducting a 'trade'.[16]

---

[14] Henderson LJ in *Samarkand Film Partnership No 3 the Revenue and Customs Commissioners* [2017] EWCA Civ 77 at [59], [2017] STC 926 at 946 and Sir Terence Atherton C in *Eclipse Film Partners No 35 LLP v Revenue and Customs Commissioners* [2015] EWCA Civ 95 at [113], [2015] STC 1429 at 1449.

[15] *Cooper (Inspector of Taxes) v C & J Clark Ltd* [1982] STC 335 Nourse J at 340.

[16] *Lewis Emanuel & Son Ltd v White (H M Inspector of Taxes)* (1965) 42 TC 369 Penycuick J at 377; *Cooper (Inspector of Taxes) v C & J Clark Ltd* [1982] STC 335 Nourse J at 340.

- A series of purchases and sales of marketable securities may amount to a trade if the transactions are carried out pursuant to a deliberate profit-making scheme.[17]

- It is easier to characterise the purchase and sale of marketable securities by a company, as compared with an individual, as being a 'trade' in marketable securities.[18]

- A degree of organisation is generally required. In the case of a professional trader; this may be nothing more than a telephone, basic bookkeeping and some capital.[19] However, it is generally wise to have a business plan and a trading strategy, however basic, particularly in the case of an individual.[20]

The lesson from these cases is that each case turns on its own facts. The determination of the tribunal of fact at first instance is crucial. The first-tier tax tribunal has to make an 'impressionistic' judgement as to whether a 'trade' exists. In practice, the tribunal of fact has a wide discretion as to whether a particular activity constitutes a 'trade' and their decision is difficult to challenge on appeal.

The taxpayer in *Cooper (Inspector of Taxes) v C & J Clark Ltd*[21] had placed surplus monies with an external broker in the hope of earning a greater return than was available by putting money on deposit in a bank account. The external broker had executed a series of thirteen trades over nine months, with the taxpayer incurring a global loss over this period of around £100,000. The tribunal at first instance considered that the taxpayer was not 'trading'. On appeal, Nourse J considered that the conclusion that the tribunal had come to was one that was open to them and he was not prepared to overturn this decision on the basis that it displayed an error of law.

In *Salt v Chamberlain (Inspector of Taxes)*[22] the taxpayer, an operational research consultant, utilised powerful computer systems to solve complex business problems. Outside of work, he used this expertise to develop a system to trade shares. Over a period of 4½ years he executed around 200 transactions, mainly in put and call options, in accordance with this system. The tribunal at first instance considered that his activity did not amount to a 'trade'. Oliver J on appeal considered that it was open to the tribunal to reach this conclusion on the facts and that he could discern no error of law by which he could overturn the decision.[23]

---

[17] *Cooper (Inspector of Taxes) v C & J Clark Ltd* [1982] STC 335 Nourse J at 340.
[18] Ibid. Nourse J at 340.
[19] *Wannell v Rothwell (Inspector of Taxes)* [1996] STC 450 Robert Walker J at 461.
[20] *Ali v HMRC* [2016] UKFTT 8 Judge Citron and Mrs Newns at [28] accepted the business plan of the taxpayer articulated orally. Of course, a business plan should ideally be in writing and contain all the usual matters that one would expect to see in a business plan such a detailed industry analysis, detailed financial projections etc.
[21] [1982] STC 335.
[22] [1979] STC 750.
[23] *Salt v Chamberlain (Inspector of Taxes)* [1979] STC 750 Oliver J at 760.

More recently, in the case of *Dr K M A Manzur v HMRC*[24] the taxpayer, a retired surgeon, utilised around £160,000 to execute around 240–300 transactions in shares via an online broker. The tribunal, in that case, considered that his activities did not amount to a 'trade'. The tribunal came to this conclusion because he had not conducted his activities in the manner of those who operated established share trading businesses.

However, in another recent case, *Ali v HMRC*[25] the taxpayer managed to convince the tribunal that his share trading activities amounted to a 'trade'. The taxpayer, in that case, ran a successful pharmacy business. He got someone in to run his pharmacy business, and he moved into an office above the pharmacy where he ran a share trading business full time. He ran the business with minimum formality and expense. He had no written business plan but articulated an oral business plan at the tribunal. His strategy was to buy and sell fast moving stocks and make a profit. He engaged in short term trading executing between four and ten transactions a day. He largely based his decisions to purchase and sell shares based on broker research reports. However, despite the taxpayer's lack of sophistication, the tribunal still considered he was conducting a 'trade'.[26]

Finally, the recent case of *Thomson and others v HMRC*[27] is a good example of a case where a taxpayer was found not to be conducting a 'trade' in CFDs because of the complete lack of sophistication in the way he purchased and sold CFD's. In that case, the court found that the taxpayer's judgement as to which CFDs he would buy and sell was 'amateurish and impressionistic'.[28] The taxpayer depended largely on information he gleaned from the financial press and friends about which CFDs he would buy and sell, and the tribunal ultimately considered that Mr Mungavin's activities did not amount to a 'trade'.[29]

WHEN IS A TAXPAYER WHO PURCHASES AND SELLS CRYPTOCURRENCY CONDUCTING A 'TRADE'?

4.6   Obviously, each case will turn on its own facts.

There are hedge funds which are active in the cryptocurrency markets, and they are likely to be able to maintain they are conducting a trade because of the scale of their organisation, and presumably because they are using a sophisticated strategy to trade in these markets.

---

[24] [2010] UKFTT 580 (TC).
[25] [2016] SFTD 335.
[26] Ibid Judge Citron and Mrs Newns at 349.
[27] [2018] UKFTT 396 (TC).
[28] Ibid Judge Jonathan Richards and Elizabeth Bridge at 255.
[29] Ibid Judge Jonathan Richards and Elizabeth Bridge at 255.

An example of an individual taxpayer who would have a good case for maintaining that they were conducting a 'trade' in cryptocurrency is one who purchases and sells cryptocurrency according to a deliberate strategy, for instance, arbitraging the price of a cryptocurrency across different exchanges. Ideally, some basic bookkeeping should also be maintained.

There may be other examples of taxpayers who could argue they have a 'trade' in cryptocurrency. Ideally, a taxpayer who wants to maintain they are 'trading' in cryptocurrency should be able to show:

(1)   They have a deliberate trading strategy, the more sophisticated the better. For instance, arbitraging a cryptocurrency on different exchanges is an example of a strategy that would qualify. A 'pairs' trading strategy could potentially qualify depending on the circumstances. A less sophisticated strategy based on 'crypto broker' research or 'charting' could also potentially qualify as 'trading' depending on the circumstances.

(2)   They execute transactions in line with this strategy.

(3)   They maintain some basic bookkeeping.

(4)   They have a business plan. Ideally, a written business plan, although it is possible to articulate an oral business plan at the first-tier tax tribunal if it comes to this, as the taxpayer in *Ali v HMRC*[30] demonstrated.

Realistically, for many taxpayers seeking to argue that they are trading in cryptocurrency before the first-tier tax tribunal, the decision could go either way. As the judgments in the share 'trading' cases above illustrate, different judges can legitimately reach different views on cases with similar facts. Appellate courts generally grant the first-tier tribunal a wide discretion in making a judgment about whether a taxpayer was 'trading' or not. They can only overturn a decision of the first-tier tribunal for an error of law, but they can't embark on a reappraisal of the facts.

In the case of the purchase and sale of cryptocurrency, it is likely to be harder for a taxpayer to maintain that a 'trade' is being carried on, as compared with a taxpayer trading shares. Cryptocurrencies have no intrinsic value, and there is no way to value them.[31] Many of the strategies being employed by individual traders are unlikely to be sophisticated. As the share 'trading' cases above illustrate, although an unsophisticated strategy is not fatal to a finding that a taxpayer is conducting a 'trade', it does make such a finding more difficult.

---

[30] [2016] SFTD 335.
[31] https://www.ft.com/content/49165b56-2dea-11e9-8744-e7016697f225.

Chapter 5

Could cryptocurrency profits be tax-free on the basis the taxpayer was 'gambling'?

Focus

From a factual point of view, it is likely to be difficult for most taxpayers to sustain an argument that they are 'gambling' in cryptocurrency/cryptoassets because:

1   They would need to trade almost blindly to have any hope of sustaining this argument.
2   Cryptoasset markets are more sophisticated than they were a few years ago. A 'gambling' argument is hard to sustain in this environment.

From a legal point of view, the argument that gains could be 'gambling' gains and tax-free is illusory:

1   From an income tax perspective, authority for such an argument is sparse. There also isn't a single case that the taxpayer has won on this argument.
2   Even if a taxpayer successfully argued that there was such an exemption for income tax purposes, they will almost certainly be caught by the capital gains tax legislation. A review of the history of the introduction of the exemption in *Taxation of Chargeable Gains Act 1992 ('TCGA'), s 5(1)* suggests that it was never intended to apply to 'gambling' in shares or cryptocurrency.

5.1   There isn't a single case about income tax in which a taxpayer has succeeded with the argument that they were 'gambling' in shares and that therefore their profits should be tax-free.

In the recent case of *Ali v HMRC*,[1] HMRC lost an argument that a taxpayer's trading losses should have been denied deductibility on the basis that they were 'gambling' losses.

There is limited authority for the proposition that the purchase and sale of shares could be 'gambling' transactions, and presumably, any profits would be tax-free.

---

[1] [2016] SFTD 335.

It is pertinent to consider these authorities as they offer the best guidance as to whether a purchase and sale of cryptocurrency could be a 'gambling' transaction that is free of tax.

The main authority to support this proposition comes from observations in the obiter of Pennycuick J in *Lewis Emanuel & Son, Ltd v White (H M Inspector of Taxes)*:[2]

> 'The word 'speculation' is not, I think, as a matter of language, an accurate antithesis either to the word 'trade' or to the word 'investment': either a trade or an investment may be speculative. On the other hand, it is certainly true, at any rate in the case of an individual, that he may carry out a whole range of financial activities which do not amount to a trade but which could equally not be described as an investment, even upon a short-term basis. These activities include betting and gambling in the narrow sense. They also include, it seems to me, all sorts of Stock Exchange transactions. For want of a better phrase, I will describe this class of activities as gambling transactions: see Graham v Green, 9 TC 309, for an analysis of these transactions in relation to an individual who made a living from betting.'[3]

Pennycuick J continued:

> 'It seems to me, however, that in general it is much more difficult to bring the activities of the company within this class of gambling transactions.'[4]

There has not yet been a case where a taxpayer has successfully argued that the profits that they made from the sale of shares were gambling profits and therefore tax-free.

In the recent case of *Ali v HMRC*,[5] the facts of which are outlined at **4.5**, HMRC lost an argument that the taxpayer was 'gambling' and that their losses should not be trading losses on this basis. In that case, the taxpayer was 'self-taught', had a very basic trading strategy largely based around broker research and recited a simple business plan orally at trial. The taxpayer undertook four to ten transactions per day and was, essentially, 'day trading'. However, the tribunal was not prepared to find that he was 'gambling' in relation to share transactions that he entered into.

In a different context, in the much older case of *Cooper (Inspector of Taxes) v Stubbs*,[6] the Court of Appeal rejected the taxpayer's argument that the profits from a number of speculative 'cotton futures' contracts that he entered into were 'gambling' profits for tax purposes. The taxpayer, in that case, was a partner in a firm of cotton brokers and merchants. In the usual course of business, partners of the firm would enter into cotton futures contracts to hedge themselves against the movement in the price of cotton that they had physically purchased

---

[2] 42 TC 369.
[3] *Lewis Emanuel & So, Ltd v White (H M Inspector of Taxes)* 42 TC 369 at Pennycuick J at 377.
[4] Ibid. Pennycuick J at 378.
[5] [2016] UKFTT 8.
[6] [1925] All ER Rep 643.

and would later sell. The taxpayer, with the knowledge of the other partners, in his own personal capacity, entered into around 50 to 60 cotton futures contracts per year that had nothing to do with hedging. He was effectively speculating. Over three consecutive income years, he made decent profits.

At first instance, the Commissioners had determined that these particular transactions did not form part of a trade and were 'gambling' transactions that were not taxable. However, on further appeal to the Court of Appeal, Pollock MR considered that the taxpayer's activities clearly amounted to a 'trade' and rejected an argument that they were 'gambling' transactions.[7] Warrington LJ with whom Atkin LJ agreed, observed that the contracts entered in to were ordinary commercial contracts, the profits generated were regular and considerable, and while the taxpayer may have been speculating and subjectively considered these transactions to be 'gambling', they were contracts entered in to by a man with skill, knowledge and experience in that market.[8] Warrington LJ therefore considered that the profits were taxable as profits or gains under the former provisions of *Income Tax 1918, Sch D, Case IV* firmly rejecting the argument that the transactions were 'gambling' transactions that were not subject to tax.

In summary, the authority to support an argument that a taxpayer can 'gamble' in shares and realise tax-free profits for income tax purposes is scarce.

ANALYSIS FROM A FACTUAL AND LEGAL POINT OF VIEW ON WHETHER A TAXPAYER COULD 'GAMBLE' IN CRYPTOCURRENCY

5.2   From a factual point of view, a taxpayer can arguably 'bet' on the stock market or cryptocurrency in the same way that they can 'bet' on a horse race or roulette. However, from a factual point of view, this argument would not be easy to sustain:

(1)   The 'share trading' cases above suggest that a taxpayer would have to trade cryptocurrency almost blindly to establish this from a factual point of view. There seemed to be an acknowledgement in the authorities above that many investments could be described as 'speculative', but that something more than 'speculation' would be needed to establish that a taxpayer was 'gambling' in cryptocurrency or shares.

(2)   The cryptocurrency market is now more sophisticated than it was in its early days. There is a greater variety of products and investments on offer, and there is more information available on investment and trading strategies. There are also professional traders such as hedge funds who are active in these markets that presumably have quite sophisticated strategies.

---

[7] Ibid at All ER Rep 643 Pollock MR at 650.
[8] Ibid at All ER Rep 643 Warrington LJ at 652 and Atkin LJ at 656.

However, there are still also potentially good arguments that a taxpayer was 'gambling' in cryptocurrency:

(1) There are many unsophisticated investors transacting in this market, and some don't even have a basic strategy.

(2) Many commentators have observed that cryptocurrency markets like Bitcoin are a 'bubble'.[9] This in itself makes it more likely that there are taxpayers who are 'gambling' in these markets.

There is little guidance on how a tribunal might make a finding that a taxpayer was 'gambling'. The principles espoused at **4.1, 4.2** and **4.3** that are used to establish whether a taxpayer is conducting a 'trade' are directly applicable to establishing whether a taxpayer is 'gambling'.

Presumably, it would first be necessary to establish that a taxpayer subjectively intended to 'gamble' throughout the time that they executed the relevant cryptocurrency transactions. Then it would be necessary to establish that the taxpayer's 'gambling' motive squared with the other facts and circumstances of the transactions, viewed objectively. In relation to these circumstances, the less organised and the less sophisticated the taxpayer is, the better.

There is probably greater scope for an argument that a particular taxpayer is 'gambling' in these markets in the sense described by Pennycuick J in *Lewis Emanuel & Co* (see **5.1**) than as compared with the share market.

The overall judgement would be an 'impressionistic' one that the transactions were 'gambling' as compared with trading or investment transactions.

The determination of the first-tier tax tribunal as to whether the taxpayer is 'gambling' will be crucial. As is seen above, it is very difficult to challenge the fact finding of the first-tier tax tribunal on appeal.

Finally, it should be pointed out that it is a concern that there is scant authority as to whether it is possible to 'gamble' in shares in the sense that any profits realised could be tax-free. From an income tax point of view, authority is scarce, and any argument is weak.

In sum, it is likely to be difficult from both a factual and a legal point of view to sustain an argument that a taxpayer was 'gambling' in cryptocurrency and that their profits should be free from income tax or corporation tax.

---

[9] For example see Kate Rooney at https://www.cnbc.com/2018/10/11/roubini-bitcoin-is-mother-of-all-scams.html where Nouriel Roubini says 'Bitcoin is the mother of all scams'

ARE GAINS FROM 'GAMBLING' IN CRYPTOCURRENCY EXEMPT FROM CAPITAL GAINS TAX?

5.3   Based on the analysis at **7.1**, cryptocurrency will be 'property' for the purposes of *TCGA 1992, s 21(2)* and therefore potentially subject to be taxed as a capital gain unless an exception applies.

The exemption from capital gains tax for 'betting' is contained in *TCGA 1992, s 51(1)* and states:

'51 Exemption for winnings and damages etc

(1)   It is hereby declared that winnings from betting, including pool betting, or lotteries or games with prizes are not chargeable gains, and no chargeable gain or allowable loss shall accrue on the disposal of rights to winnings obtained by participating in any pool betting or lottery or game with prizes.'

The wording of this exemption was precisely the same as the wording of the exemption when it was introduced by *Finance Act 1965, s 27(7)*, which introduced capital gains tax.[10]

Essentially, there is a real question as to whether this section was intended to be restricted to 'betting' in the more narrow sense of 'betting' on a horse race or participating in a lottery or whether it was meant to be interpreted in a wider sense as applying to 'gambling' on the share market or on cryptocurrency transactions.

The Oxford English Dictionary states that 'winnings' means:

'money won, especially by gambling'.

The Oxford English Dictionary states that 'betting' means:

'the action of gambling money on the outcome of a race, game, or other unpredictable event.'

Certainly, it is possible to construe profits from 'gambling' in cryptocurrency or shares as being 'winnings from betting' on a plain English interpretation of those words.

However, a broader consideration of:

(1)   the wording of *TCGA 1992, s 51(1)*; and
(2)   the that *Finance Act 1962* introduced income tax on short-term gains, which was in force and extended by *Finance Act 1965*, is the same piece of legislation that introduced capital gains tax and the exemption for 'winnings from betting';

---

[10] The exact same wording was also reflected in *Capital Gains Tax Act 1979, s 19(4)* that consolidated the capital gains tax legislation at that time.

tends toward the conclusion that *TCGA 1992, s 51(1)* refers to 'betting' in the more colloquial sense of betting on a horse race or a lottery, rather than betting on shares or cryptocurrency/ cryptoassets.

TCGA 1992, s 51(1)

5.4 The opening words of *TCGA 1992, s 51(1)* adopt an inclusive definition:

'winnings from betting, including pool betting, or lotteries or games with prizes are not chargeable gains … …'

The context would suggest that the legislature intended to restrict the exemption to 'gambling' in the colloquial sense of betting on horse racing, lotteries and the like.

The second part of *TCGA 1992, s 51(1)* clearly does not apply to 'gambling' in shares or cryptocurrency at all:

'and no chargeable gain or allowable loss shall accrue on the disposal of rights to winnings obtained by participating in any pool betting or lottery or game with prizes.'

Most of the Hansard debate on this section focuses on 'betting' or 'gambling' in the colloquial sense.[11]

Finance Act 1962 **and the taxation of short-term gains**

5.5 *Finance Act 1962* introduced a short-term gains tax. Essentially, it subjected gains:

(1)   on land made within three years; and
(2)   gains on all other assets within six months;

to income tax under the new *Schedule D Case VII*. Plainly, it was introduced with the particular intention of taxing gains made by speculators.[12]

Finance Act 1965, s 17(1) effected changes to the short-term gains tax legislation in *Finance Act* 1962, such that intangible assets such as shares were subject to the income tax charge under *Schedule D Case VII* where they were bought and sold within 12 months. Again, very plainly, the legislation intended to tax activity of individuals who were 'gambling'

---

[11] Hansard vol [712] col 47 (10 May 1965) and vol 713 cols 893–914 (27 May 1965), with the one exception being a reference to 'gambling' on the stock market at vol 713 col 910 (27 May 1965).
[12] See also Hansard vol [658] col 1344 (3 May 1962).

or 'speculating' in shares.[13] Although speculative gains that were subject to income tax under *Schedule D Case VII* were specifically exempted from the capital gains tax legislation,[14] Parliament could not, therefore, have intended that short term speculative gains on shares bought and sold within 12 months could ever have fallen with the "gambling" exemption in *TCGA 1992, s 27(2)* when they introduced this section. In relation to speculative gains made on shares bought and sold over a period of greater than 12 months, it is hard to conceive that Parliament would have intended that such speculative gains from trading in shares that were subject to the capital gains tax legislation in *Finance Act 1965* should obtain the benefit of the 'betting' exemption that was introduced in *Finance Act 1965, s 27(7)*.

Furthermore, when Parliament repealed the short term gains legislation in 1971 in the interest of simplicity and reform, the capital gains tax provisions in *Finance Act 1965* would take over taxing these short-term gains.[15] In sum, the drafters evidenced no intention at this time to exempt from capital gains tax gains derived from speculating or 'gambling' in shares or other intangible assets.

In summary, interpreting the exemption for 'betting' in what is now *TCGA 1992, s 51(1)* in a purposive way, on balance it seems that it was never the intention of Parliament that 'gambling' in shares or other intangible assets should obtain the benefit of this exemption. The better view is that this exemption is confined to 'betting' and 'gambling' in the colloquial sense, such as horse racing, lotteries and the like.

Therefore, even if a taxpayer managed to persuade a court that they should not be subject to income tax on the basis that they were 'gambling' in shares or cryptoassets, that taxpayer would most likely be subject to tax under the capital gains tax legislation.

In sum, the argument that a taxpayer can realise a gain tax-free on the basis that they are 'gambling' in shares or cryptoassets is illusory.

---

[13] To the extent that it may be allowable to refer to Hansard, the Hansard debate tends to confirm that it was the intention of Parliament to subject to income tax, in particular, individual making speculative gains from trading in shares: Hansard, Vol [713] cols 66, 76, 114 (24 May 1965) in particular.

[14] *Finance Act 1965, Sch 6, para 3.*

[15] To the extent that it is permissible to look at Hansard, see in particular, Hansard, Standing Committee H, House of Commons, cols 652–655, 659 and 662 (16 June 1971).

Chapter 6

Could cryptocurrency profits be 'miscellaneous income'?

6.1   There may be cases where a taxpayer's activity falls short of 'trading' but is sufficiently frequent that it could be considered to be 'miscellaneous income' within *Income Tax (Trading and Other Income) Act 2005 ('ITTOIA 2005'), s 687*.[1] Essentially, this was what the majority of the court in *Cooper (Inspector of Taxes) v Stubbs*[2] found in relation to a taxpayer who was speculating on cotton futures transactions in a capacity as an individual, as compared with the trades he conducted as a partner in a cotton brokerage firm.

The 'miscellaneous income' provisions are wider than the former *Schedule D Case VI* provisions. *ITTOIA 2005, s 687* states:

> '687 Charge to tax on income not otherwise charge
>
> (1)   Income tax is charged under this Chapter on income from any source that is not charged to income tax under or as a result of any other provision of this Act or any other Act.
>
> (2)   Subsection (1) does not apply to annual payments.'

Most of the authorities in relation to *ITTOIA 2005, s 687* were decided under the old *Schedule D Case VI* provisions. They are not particularly detailed as to when a sum received will constitute 'income' for the purposes of those provisions.

However, it is clear that *ITTOIA 2005, s 687* is wider in scope than *Schedule D Case VI*. However, it is not clear what the demarcation is between a 'non-trading' transaction that is 'income' and falls within *ITTOIA 2005, s 687* and a 'non-trading' transaction that is simply subject to the capital gains tax provisions. Based on historical precedent, it will be a relatively small number of 'non-trading' transactions that fall within *ITTOIA 2005, s 687*.

---

[1] *ITTOIA 2005, ss 687–689*. These sections are commonly known as the 'sweep up' provisions and replaced the former *Schedule D Case VI* category of chargeable income.
[2] [1925] All ER Rep 643 Warrington LJ at 652 and Atkin LJ at 656.

Chapter 7

Cryptocurrency – an investment?

Focus

There is no question that cryptocurrency and cryptoassets are 'property' for the purposes of '*TCGA 1992, s 21(1)* because they represent something that can be 'turned to account'.

Therefore, cryptocurrency and cryptoassets can potentially be subject to tax under the capital gains tax legislation.

If cryptocurrency/cryptoasset gains or losses are already classified as trading gains/trading losses, they will not be subject to capital gains tax treatment.

For reasons given below, cryptocurrency/cryptoassets gains and losses are unlikely to fall within the exemption for 'betting' in *TCGA 1992, s 51(1)*.

Regard needs to be had to the capital gains tax pooling rules in calculating any gains.

DOES THE CAPITAL GAINS TAX LEGISLATION APPLY TO CRYPTOCURRENCY GAINS AND LOSSES?

7.1 First, it is pertinent to consider whether the capital gains tax rules apply to cryptocurrency.

Capital gains tax is payable by a person, corporate or individual, where they dispose of an 'asset' (*TCGA 1992, s 1(1)*).

All forms of property are stated to be assets (*TCGA 1992, s 21(1)*):

'(1) All forms of property shall be assets for the purposes of this Act, were situated in the United Kingdom or not, including –

   (a) Options, debts, and incorporeal property generally, and

   (b) Currency, with the exception (subject to express provision to the contrary) of sterling;

   (c) Any form of property created by the person disposing of it, or otherwise coming to be owned without being acquired.'

This then raises the question of what is an 'asset' and what is 'property' for the purposes of these provisions.

The leading case on this matter is the 1979 decision of the House of Lords in *O'Brien (Inspector of Taxes' Appellant v Benson's Hosiery (Holdings) Ltd. Respondent.*[1]

O'Brien v HMRC[2] concerned a taxpayer company that had entered into a personal services contract for the sale and marketing services of one of its directors for a period of seven years. The director was released from his obligations around five years early for the payment of a capital sum of £50,000. The taxpayer company was originally assessed to tax on the £50,000 receipt on the basis that they had disposed of an asset by giving up their rights under the personal service contract.[3]

The taxpayer company was successful at first instance before the Special Commissioners, but this decision was reversed by Fox J in the High Court. On further appeal, the Court of Appeal stated that the meaning of 'asset' was a 'wide one'.[4] However, the Court of Appeal ultimately agreed with the taxpayer company that the application of the capital gains tax legislation was entirely inappropriate. They held that the opening words of *Finance Act 1965, s 22(1)* clearly indicated that the term 'asset' must be 'some form of property',[5] because the scheme of the legislation implied that an asset must be something with a 'market value'[6] and because a contract for personal services could not be transferred, it could not have a market value and therefore could not be an asset for the purposes of *Finance Act 1965, s 22(1).*[7]

On further appeal, the House of Lords overturned the Court of Appeal's decision and allowed HMRC's appeal. Lord Russell of Killowen, giving judgment for the court, espoused that:

> 'It was contended for the taxpayer that the rights of an employer under a contract of service were not 'property' nor an 'asset' of the employer, because they cannot be turned to account by transfer or assignment to another. But in my opinion this contention supposes a restricted view of the scheme of the imposition of the capital gains tax which the statutory language does not permit. If, as here, the employer is able to exact from the employee a substantial sum as a term of releasing him from his obligations to serve, the rights of the employer appear to me to bear quite sufficiently the mark of an asset of the employer, something which he can turn to account, notwithstanding that his ability to turn it to account is by a type of disposal limited by the nature of the asset.'[8]

[1] [1980] AC 562 (1979).
[2] Ibid.
[3] The assessment was made under what was then *Finance Act 1965, ss 19, 22(1), (3)*. These provisions are substantially the same as s *TCGA 1992, ss 1(1), 21(1), 22.*
[4] *O'Brien (Inspector of Taxes' Appellant v Benson's Hosiery (Holdings) Limited* [1978] 3 WLR 609 at 622 per Buckley LJ giving judgment for the court.
[5] Ibid at Buckley LJ giving judgment for the court 619.
[6] Ibid at Buckley LJ giving judgment for the court 620.
[7] Ibid at Buckley LJ giving judgment for the court 621.
[8] *O'Brien (Inspector of Taxes' Appellant v Benson's Hosiery (Holdings) Ltd Respondent* [1980] A.C. 562 (1979) Lord Russell of Killoween at 573.

In short, the House of Lords took an extremely broad view of what constituted an 'asset' for the purposes of the capital gains tax legislation. Essentially, they considered that the taxpayer company 'turning to account' its rights under a personal services contract by surrendering them for £50,000, constituted the disposal of an asset for the purposes of the capital gains tax legislation.

Impliedly, they also considered that the term 'property' for the purposes of *TCGA 1992* was very wide and included things which may not be 'property' at common law.

There is little doubt that the sale of cryptocurrency by a taxpayer would constitute the disposal of an asset. A taxpayer holding cryptocurrency, through their ownership of a private key, effectively has the right to deal with that cryptocurrency. This right has value because other people are prepared to pay to acquire a taxpayer's cryptocurrency. Bitcoin and many other cryptocurrencies even have a market value that can be discovered on an exchange or marketplace. There can be little question that the taxpayer is 'turning to account' a valuable right, be that right personal or proprietary, and this will clearly be the disposal of an asset for the purposes of the capital gains tax legislation.[9]

CRYPTOCURRENCY – AN INVESTMENT?

7.2   Based on the analysis above, every sale of cryptocurrency will be subject to capital gains tax unless an exception or relief applies.

There are exceptions where:

(1)   the profit has already been subject to 'income tax', that is where the taxpayer has established that they are 'trading' profits; and
(2)   for 'betting' transactions.[10]

As stated at **5.3–5.5** the better view is that 'betting' or 'gambling' in *TCGA 1992, s 51(1)* refers to 'betting' or 'gambling' in the colloquial sense and does not apply to 'betting' or 'gambling' in cryptocurrency or shares.

Therefore, unless a taxpayer is conducting a 'trade', then the taxpayer will be holding cryptocurrency as an 'investment' that will be subject to capital gains tax in accordance with *TCGA 1992*.

---

[9] *TCGA 1992, s 1(1)* in conjunction with *s 21(1)*.
[10] *TCGA 1992, s 51(1)*.

For most individual investors who are not trading full time, it is most likely that for tax purposes they will be holding cryptocurrency as an investment and will be subject to capital gains tax treatment on this investment.

CAPITAL GAINS TAX – SHARE POOLING RULES

7.3 Bitcoin is divisible into smaller units known as Satoshis. There are 100 million Satoshis in a single bitcoin.[11]

Individual Satoshis cannot be uniquely identified. All that can be identified is the number of Satoshis at a particular public address or the number of Satoshis that were spent in a particular transaction.[12]

These two facts may or may not be true for other cryptocurrencies.

The 'share pooling' rules apply to 'securities' (*TCGA 1992, s 104 generally*). A cryptocurrency like Bitcoin will generally fulfil the definition of 'security' in *TCGA 1992, s 104(3)(ii)* being:

> 'any other assets where they are of a nature to be dealt in without identifying the particular assets disposed of or acquired'.

Based on the above facts, Bitcoin and possibly other cryptocurrencies will satisfy the definition of 'securities' (*TCGA 1992, s 104(3)(ii)*) and therefore will be subject to the "share pooling" rules in *TCGA 1992, s 104*.

Essentially, where bitcoins are purchased and sold by a person in the same capacity (that capacity usually being as individual or trustee), there are three different types of 'pooling rules' that could potentially apply to an individual, in the following order of priority:

(1) same day purchase and sale 'pooling rules';
(2) purchase and sale of cryptocurrency occurring within 30 days of each other;[13] and
(3) general 'pooling rules' for all other transactions.

---

[11] https://medium.com/@EricGrill/the-divisibility-of-bitcoin-fc1bcb40dd52.

[12] https://bitcoin.stackexchange.com/questions/21452/can-each-bitcoin-and-satoshi-be-uniquely-identified.

[13] It should be noted that for corporation tax purposes this rule is a 10-day rule (*TCGA 1992, s 107*).

Pooling rule 1 – same day purchase and sale 'pooling rules'

7.4   Where bitcoins are purchased and sold by an individual in the same capacity *on the same day*, the bitcoins purchased are treated as being purchased in one transaction, and these same bitcoins are treated as being sold in one transaction on the same day.[14]

To the extent that the bitcoins sold on the same day exceeds the bitcoins purchased on the same day, the other pooling rules will apply in the order of priority specified above.

Example 1

12 May 2019 – Edward purchased 50 bitcoins for £5,000 each.

26 June 2019 – Edward purchased a further 10 bitcoins for £10,000 each.

26 June 2019 – Edward purchased a further 10 bitcoins for £10,050 each.

26 June 2019 – Edward later sold 30 bitcoins for £10,100 each.

Analysis

First, it can be observed that 20 bitcoins were purchased on 26 June 2019 and 30 bitcoins were later sold on this day. Bitcoins sold on 26 June 2019 exceeded the bitcoins that were purchased on that day. Therefore, pooling rule 1 applies to the purchased of 20 bitcoins on 26 June 2019 and subsequent sale of 20 bitcoins on that same day:

(1)   20 bitcoins are treated as purchased on 26 June 2019 for £200,500;

(2)   20 bitcoins are treated as sold on 26 June 2019 for £202,000;

(3)   A profit of £1,500 is yielded from the same day purchase and sale rules;

(4)   10 bitcoins are subject to the general pooling rules discussed below (*TCGA 1992, s 104):*

    (a)   The pool consisted of 50 bitcoins with a total value of £250,000 (all purchased 10 May 2019);

    (b)   10 bitcoins are treated as sold from the pool on 26 June 2019 for £101,000.

(5)   The application of the pooling rules in *TCGA 1992, s 104* yields a profit of £149,000.

Pooling rule 2 – sale and purchase of cryptocurrency occurring within 30 days

7.5   Where bitcoins are *sold and then purchased again within 30 days* by an individual in the same capacity, the bitcoins purchased are treated as being sold by the individual.[15]

---

[14] *TCGA 1992, s 105.*
[15] *TCGA 1992, s 106A.*

Pooling rules 1 and 3 will then determine the tax treatment of the sale of other bitcoins.

Example 2

12 May 2019 – Sally purchased 50 bitcoins for £5,000 each.

26 June 2019 – Sally sold 10 bitcoins £10,000 each.

28 June 2019 – Sally purchased a further 20 bitcoins on for £9,700 each.

Analysis

It can be observed that 10 bitcoins were sold on 26 June 2019 and then 10 bitcoins were purchased on 28 June 2019.

Therefore, the 2nd pooling rule applies to this transaction. The 10 bitcoins purchased on 28 June 2019 are treated as being sold on 26 June 2019 (as compared with having 10 bitcoins out of the general pool that was established on 12 May 2019 being sold).

The capital gain/loss would be calculated as follows:

(1) Consideration: 10 bitcoins sold for £10,000 each, totals £100,000.
(2) Less allowable costs (from cost at 28 June 2019): 10 bitcoins purchased at £9,700, totals £97,000.
(3) Total capital gain = £100,000 − £97,000 = £3,000.

Pooling rule 3 – general pooling rule (*TCGA 1992, s 104*)

7.6   Where bitcoins are *purchased and then sold again after more than 30 days* by an individual in the same capacity, the bitcoins purchased are pooled and treated as being one indistinguishable asset. The cost of progressively purchased cryptocurrency is treated as forming part of one single asset. A pro-rata proportion of the asset is treated as being sold each time a sale of bitcoins are made.[16]

Example 3

30 April 2019 – William purchased 50 bitcoins for £4,000 each.

13 May 2019 – William purchased 40 bitcoins £6,000 each.

3 July 2019 – William sold 30 bitcoins for £9,500 each.

---

[16] *TCGA 1992, s 104.*

Analysis

The bitcoins purchased on 30 April 2019 and 13 May 2019 are part of the same pool or a single asset.

Therefore, 90 bitcoins have a cost of $50 \times £4,000 + 40 \times £6,000 = £440,000$

On 3 July 2019, 30 of these bitcoins are sold. Their pro-rated cost is $30/90 \times £440,000 = £146,666.66$

Consideration for the 30 bitcoins sold is $30 \times £9,500 = £285,000$

Total capital gain $= £285,000 - £146,666.66 = £138,333.33$

Chapter 8

Cryptocurrency losses

Focus

In order for an individual to claim a carry forward loss as a trading loss, they need to show that they carried on a 'trade' in cryptocurrency based on the principles outlined in **Chapter 4**:

 (i) they carried on a 'trade' in cryptocurrency based on the principles outlined in **Chapter 4**;
 (ii) the trade was conducted on a 'commercial basis'; and
(iii) the trade was conducted with a 'view to the realisation of profits'.

In practice, this will mean the individual taxpayer demonstrating:

 (i) that they are conducting their cryptocurrency trading on a full-time basis;
 (ii) some sort of a trading strategy (the more formal/sophisticated the better);
(iii) that they were diligent in executing that strategy; and
(iv) that they have a business plan (ideally written – more formal the better).

WHEN CAN A CRYPTOCURRENCY LOSS BE CLAIMED AS A 'TRADING' LOSS?

8.1   First, a taxpayer must establish that are carrying on a 'trade' in line with the principles in paras **4.1–4.3**.

Secondly, *Income Tax Act 2007 ('ITA 2007'), ss 66* and *74* contain provisions that restrict relief of income tax losses from trading income unless the losses are commercial.

ITA 2007, s 66 – general restriction on utilisation of carry forward losses

ITA 2007, s 66 provides a general restriction on the utilisation of carry forward losses. It states:

> '(1)   Trade loss relief against general income for a loss made in a trade in a tax year is not available unless the trade is commercial.

(2) The trade is commercial if it is carried on throughout the basis period for the tax year—

    (a) on a commercial basis, and

    (b) with a view to the realisation of profits of the trade.

(3) If at any time a trade is carried on so as to afford a reasonable expectation of profit, it is treated as carried on at that time with a view to the realisation of profits.'

ITA 2007, s 74 – restriction of carrying back losses to use against early year trade losses

8.2   *ITA 2007, s 74* contains a restriction that applies to early trade losses. For the present purposes, it is *s 74(2)* that is chiefly relevant. It states:

(2) The trade is commercial if it is carried on throughout the basis period for the tax year—

    (a) on a commercial basis, and

    (b) in such a way that profits of the trade could reasonably be expected to be made in the basis period or within a reasonable time afterwards.

Case law on the 'commercial basis' test

8.3   Henderson LJ in *Samarkand Film Partnership No 3 and others v HMRC*[1] made some general observations about the first and second limbs that he referred to as the 'commerciality test' and the 'profitability test'. He observed that they were not mutually exclusive, and they were necessarily overlapping, and the extent to which they overlapped would vary from case to case.[2]

Robert Walker J in *Wannell v Roberts*[3] considered the meaning of the first limb 'on a commercial basis' in very similar provisions in *Finance Act 1978, s 30(4)*. He observed:

'I was not shown any authority in which the court has considered the expression 'on a commercial basis', but it was suggested that the best guide is to view 'commercial' as the antithesis of 'uncommercial', and I do find that a useful approach. A trade may be conducted in an uncommercial way either because the terms of trade are uncommercial (for instance, the hobby market-gardening enterprise where the prices of fruit and vegetables do not realistically reflect the overheads and variable costs of the enterprise) or because the way in which the trade is conducted is uncommercial in other respects (for instance, the hobby art gallery or antique shop where the opening hours are unpredictable and depend simply on the owner's convenience). *The distinction is between the serious trader who, whatever his shortcomings*

---

[1] [2017] STC 926.
[2] Ibid at 953.
[3] [1996] STC 450 at 461.

in skill, experience or capital, is seriously interested in profit, and the amateur or dilettante [Emphasis added]. There will no doubt be many difficult borderline cases well for the commissioners to decide; and such borderline cases could as well occur in Bond Street as at a car boot sale.'

Henderson LJ in *Samarkand Film Partnership No 3 and others v HMRC*[4] referred to these comments as being 'helpful' and further agreed with Robert Walker J that a 'serious interest in profit' is a hallmark of 'commerciality'.[5]

In *Wannell v Roberts*,[6] Robert Walker J heard an appeal by a taxpayer who was a former commodities trader. The taxpayer had left his former employment and began dealing on his own account with a very simple set up based at his private residence. At first instance, the Deputy Special Commissioner determined that while he was 'trading', he was not doing so on a 'commercial basis' because of 'a lack of commercial organisation'.[7]

Robert Walker J observed if by 'a lack of commercial organisation' the Deputy Special Commissioner had in mind 'office accommodation and equipment and staff'[8] the Deputy Special Commissioner would have been in error in attaching too much weight to this matter. He also expressed concern that the Deputy Special Commissioner's finding had been influenced by the lack of self-discipline or casualness in which the taxpayer had executed his trading strategy.[9] That is, he had not always executed trades in accordance with his trading strategy. Robert Walker J indicated that he would have liked more evidence on these matters to reach a conclusive view that there was an appealable error. However, with insufficient evidence on these matters, he was not prepared to find that the Deputy Special Commissioner had erred in finding that the taxpayer was not conducting his 'trade' on a 'commercial basis'.[10]

Finally, in considering the profitability test in *ITA 2007, s 66(2)(b)* Mr Justice Nugee in *Seven Individuals v HMRC*[11] considered that 'the mere fact that there is a realistic possibility of profit … does not entail that the LLP is carrying on a trade on a commercial basis.'[12] He further considered that both the likelihood and level of profitability were relevant to a consideration of whether a trade was being carried on 'on a commercial basis'.[13] He considered that 'a person seriously interested in commercial success' would be unlikely to regard a 'trade' that had a 'remote possibility of a small profit as worth carrying on as a commercial venture'.[14]

---

[4] [2017] STC 926.
[5] Ibid at 953.
[6] [1996] STC 450.
[7] Ibid at 455.
[8] Ibid at 461.
[9] Ibid at 461.
[10] Ibid at 461 and 462.
[11] [2017] UK UT 132 (TCC).
[12] [2017] UK UT 132 (TCC) at [54].
[13] Ibid.
[14] Ibid.

The requirements in *ITA 2007, ss 66(2)(b)* and *74(2)(b)*

Essentially, the better view is that:

8.4

(1)   the test 'with a view to the realisation of profits of the trade' in *ITA 2007, s 66(2)(b)* is a test that involves considering the subjective motivation of the taxpayer; and

(2)   the test in *ITA 2007, s 66(3)* that a 'trade is carried on so as to afford a reasonable expectation of profit, it will be treated as being carried on with a view to the realisation of profits' is effectively an objective override[15]

(3)   arguably, the test in *ITA 2007, s 74(2)(b)* 'in such a way that profits of the trade could reasonably be expected to be made in the basis period or within a reasonable time afterwards' should also be an objective test.[16]

WHEN COULD A CRYPTOCURRENCY LOSS BE CLAIMED AS A 'TRADING LOSS'?

8.5   First, a taxpayer must establish that are carrying on a 'trade' in line with the principles in **4.1–4.3**.

A taxpayer would need to establish that they conducted their trade on a 'commercial basis' in line with the principles espoused by Robert Walker J in *Wannell v Roberts*.[17] Essentially, a taxpayer trading cryptocurrency would need to demonstrate:

1   A clear trading strategy that they stuck to, based on the 'share trading' cases above at **4.5**. An obvious example of a trading strategy would be arbitraging a cryptocurrency between different exchanges. It is possible for a taxpayer to maintain that they are trading with a less sophisticated strategy. For instance, in the case of *Ali v HMRC*,[18] the taxpayer was found to be 'trading' with a simple strategy based on broker research reports. As stated above, whether there is a 'trade' is very much an impressionistic judgment that is made by the first-tier tax tribunal. Generally, the more sophisticated the trading strategy, the better. Depending on the circumstances, it may be possible for a 'pairs' trading strategy to qualify.

2   Ideally that they were trading on a full-time basis.

3   Basic office equipment such as a desk and a computer.

4   Basic bookkeeping.

---

[15] *Ingenious Games LLP v HMRC* [2019] UKUT 0226 (TCC) Mrs Justice Falk and Judge Tim Herrington at [315].

[16] This is supported by decisions under the predecessor *ICTA 1988, ss 384* (now *ITA 2007, s 66(2)(b)*) and *381* (now *ITA 2007, s 74(2)(b)*). See *Walls v Livesey (Inspector of Taxes)* [1995] STC (SCD) 12 at [6].

[17] [1996] STC 450 at 461.

[18] [2016] UKFTT 8 (TC).

As above, the judgment of the first-tier tribunal as to whether a taxpayer is conducting a trade on a 'commercial basis' is largely impressionistic. The more sophisticated the trading strategy and the more disciplined the taxpayer is in sticking to that strategy, the better.

A decision of the first-tier tribunal as to whether a taxpayer is conducting a trade on a 'commercial basis' is typically difficult to challenge on appeal.

Chapter 9

Cryptocurrency 'mining'

Focus

Bitcoin or cryptocurrency 'mined' by an individual may be either:

(i) 'trading' income – where the taxpayer has a sufficient degree or organisation based on the principles in **Chapter 4**. That is, the taxpayer:

    (a) can articulate a business plan; and

    (b) conducts 'mining' in such a way as to maximise their profit; or

(ii) 'miscellaneous' income – where they 'mine' on a more casual basis that is insufficient to amount to a trade.

WHAT IS BITCOIN/CRYPTOCURRENCY MINING?

9.1 As outlined at **3.8**, the Bitcoin network has special nodes known as 'miner' nodes. These nodes perform a crucial function in relation to the 'consensus mechanism' by which all nodes on the network agree that a certain transaction has taken place.

Essentially, these nodes compete to solve a complex mathematical problem, known as a 'proof of work', that is generated each time a participant on the network wishes to transfer bitcoins.

The miner who successfully solves the puzzle is rewarded with bitcoins. Through 2019, this reward was 12.5 bitcoins per block solved.[1] Based on a price of £9,500 per bitcoin, this would mean a reward of approximately £118,750. However, the reward for solving a block is reduced as time goes on, and halves roughly every four years. The price is expected to halve again in 2020.[2] A miner may also receive a discretionary fee as an incentive, paid in bitcoin by the party initiating the transaction.

---

[1] https://medium.com/coinmonks/blockchain-consensus-and-fault-tolerance-in-a-nutshell-765de83b8d03; https://bitcoinvox.com/bitcoin-mining-profitable/.
[2] https://www.coindesk.com/information/how-bitcoin-mining-works.

There are two crucial elements to mining bitcoin profitably:

(1) investing in a quality computer hardware, known as a 'mining rig', to give one the best chance of solving the 'proof of work' and therefore maximise revenues; and

(2) access to a cheap source of power for the 'mining rig' in order to minimise expenses.[3]

A Bitcoin miner typically joins a 'pool' of miners who share the rewards of their mining efforts. This helps smooth revenues, as there is a great deal of luck in solving the cryptographic puzzle that is generated each time a user wishes to transfer bitcoins.

WHEN WILL BITCOIN/CRYPTOCURRENCY RECEIVED FROM 'MINING' BE 'TRADING' INCOME?

9.2   The principles outlined in **Chapter 4** establish when a taxpayer will be carrying on a 'trade'. Essentially, a Bitcoin miner will need to establish that:

(1) they have invested in a quality 'mining rig'; and

(2) their activities are sufficiently organised.

In relation to (2), ideally, an individual miner would be able to articulate a simple business plan, demonstrate basic bookkeeping and also demonstrate that they were running their business in a way that maximised profit. This would most likely mean joining a 'mining pool' and trying to run their business in a way that minimised energy costs.

However, it is likely to be the scale and organisation of a Bitcoin miner's activity that ultimately determine whether they can be said to be 'trading'. A Bitcoin miner operating a single rig that effectively operates autonomously is likely to struggle to convenience HMRC that they are 'trading'. At the other end of the spectrum, a 'mining farm' that employs hundreds of rigs in a data centre should have no trouble at all convincing HMRC that they are 'trading'. Each case will turn on its own facts.

Where revenues received by a miner were not 'trading income', they would almost certainly be 'miscellaneous income'.[4] It is highly unlikely that 'mining' activity would be considered to be a hobby or otherwise 'private' in nature.

---

[3] https://www.thebalance.com/can-bitcoin-mining-make-a-profit-4157922.
[4] See **Chapter 6**.

WHEN CAN TRADING LOSSES FROM 'MINING' BE CLAIMED?

9.3   As per **Chapter 5**, to be able to claim carry forward trading losses for up to four years after the losses were made, an individual 'miner' would need to demonstrate that they carried on their trade:

(a)   on a commercial basis; and

(b)   with a view to the realisation of profits of the trade.[5]

The four-year carry back trade loss relief provisions that allow a loss to be carried back in the first four year of the trade contain a further requirement in relation to limb (b) that profits could reasonably be expected to be made in the year that the loss was incurred, or within a reasonable time afterwards.[6]

First, an individual 'miner' will need to demonstrate that they were carrying on a 'trade', as discussed at **9.2**. If these requirements are satisfied, it is most likely that the individual miner' will satisfy the requirements for 'trade loss' relief. Essentially, the individual 'miner' should be able to:

(1)   demonstrate that they invested in a quality 'mining' rig;

(2)   demonstrate that they joined a 'mining pool';

(3)   articulate at least a simple business plan (a formal written plan is always better); and

(4)   demonstrate that they ran their business in a way that maximised revenues and minimised energy costs.

---

[5] *ITA 2007, s 66(2)(a).*
[6] *ITA 2007, s 74(2).*

Chapter 10

Airdrop cryptoassets/tokens

Focus

Airdropped cryptoassets/tokens are received by a taxpayer, usually for free. Airdrops are often used to gain widespread support for a project.

Typically, a user will not be subject to income tax or corporation tax on the airdropped cryptoassets where they have not done anything to receive them.

A taxpayer may potentially be subject to income tax or corporation tax, where the airdropped cryptoassets are incidental to a trade of a taxpayer.

Airdropped cryptoassets are likely to be subject to capital gains tax when sold, or income tax/ corporate tax if they relate to a trade of the taxpayer.

WHAT ARE 'AIRDROPS'?

10.1   Airdrops involve giving cryptocurrency/cryptoassets to a taxpayer for free. The purpose of an airdrop is to try and gain widespread support for a project.

There are two main ways a taxpayer may receive an airdrop:

(1)   Through signing up for the airdrop via bulletin boards, or a social media newsletter.
(2)   Unsolicited airdrops where a taxpayer automatically receives cryptocurrency/cryptoassets because the taxpayer holds a certain value of cryptocurrency, for instance, on the Ethereum network.

WHAT ARE THE INCOME TAX/CORPORATE TAX CONSEQUENCES OF AN 'AIRDROP'?

10.2   A taxpayer who receives airdropped cryptocurrency/cryptoassets will generally not be subject to income tax or corporation tax on receipt of these tokens where:

(1)   the taxpayer has not done anything to receive them; and

(2)   they are not otherwise incidental to a trade.

A taxpayer may be liable for income tax or corporation tax where these airdropped cryptocurrency/cryptoassets are related to or incidental to a trade.

WHAT ARE THE TAX CONSEQUENCES WHEN A TAXPAYER SELLS AN AIRDROPPED CRYPTOASSET?

10.3   A taxpayer who receives an airdropped cryptoasset that was not connected with a trade is likely to be subject to capital gains tax on the sale of that cryptoasset.

A taxpayer who receives cryptoassets that are incidental to a trade of the taxpayer may potentially be subject to income tax or corporation tax on any profit made from the sale of these cryptoassets.

Chapter 11

Forks in the Blockchain and their tax consequences

Focus

An accidental fork occurs where the Blockchain temporarily splits into two branches. An accidental fork occurs occasionally. The most common reason for an accidental fork is that two different 'miners' solve the cryptographic puzzle for verifying a block at roughly the same time. The Blockchain should generally revert relatively quickly to a single branch. An accidental fork has no tax consequences.

A hard fork occurs where a significant group within the Bitcoin community decides that they want a permanent change in the Bitcoin protocol/software in order that Bitcoin better serves their particular needs. The Bitcoin community agrees to change the software such that the Blockchain forks into two different branches controlled by two different protocols.

When a hard fork occurs, a cryptocurrency holder may simply receive new cryptoassets in exchange for old cryptoassets, or they may receive a new allotment of cryptoassets in addition to their original holding of cryptoassets, with the number of new cryptoassets they receive being equal in number to their original holding. Where this happens, the allowable costs of the original assets will be split proportionately across all the cryptoassets they come to hold according to their market value as a result of the hard fork.

WHAT IS AN ACCIDENTAL 'FORK'?

11.1   An accidental fork occurs where the Blockchain for a cryptocurrency temporarily splits in two. These incidents occur occasionally. An accidental fork generally occurs where two 'miners' solve the cryptographic puzzle for verifying a block at the same time. Once a new further block is verified, this will be added to one branch of the chain and this longer branch should be the branch that is verified by a majority of nodes on the network. The shorter branch should fall away, and the Blockchain should revert to a single branch.

An accidental fork has no tax consequences for taxpayers holding cryptocurrency on the Blockchain.

WHAT IS A HARD 'FORK'?

11.2   Bitcoin and Ethereum operate as open source software projects. Changes to the software, containing the protocols by which these cryptocurrencies operate, are made by a process that involves some sort of consensus within their respective communities.

In the case of Bitcoin, any user can propose a change to the software through a Bitcoin Improvement Proposal ('BIP').[1] An editor must approve the BIP. The BIP is then voted on by the latest 2016 'miners', essentially those miners who have mined Bitcoin in the last two weeks, and 95% of these 'miners' must approve the change for the BIP to be implemented.[2] Users on the network must upgrade to the latest version of the software accordingly. It is this process that can be used to create a 'hard fork' such that the Bitcoin software Blockchain splits into two branches.

Probably the best-known example of this occurred on the Bitcoin network on 1 August 2017. Two different groups in the Bitcoin community wanted to use Bitcoin for different purposes:

(1)   The first group wanted to encourage people to use Bitcoin as a payment method. This group wanted to increase the size of blocks on the Blockchain from 1MB to 8MB to speed up transaction processing times. This group tended not to be so concerned about the price of Bitcoin.

(2)   The second group held Bitcoin for trading or investment and were primarily concerned about the price of Bitcoin and less concerned about transaction processing time. They were generally happy with the 1MB block size, and a smaller block size also meant nodes required less processing power to verify transactions and therefore resulting in lower electricity costs in verifying blocks.[3]

A BIP was put forward by the first group to create a 'hard fork' in the Blockchain. This split the Blockchain in two and created two new cryptocurrencies, Bitcoin Cash and Bitcoin SV. Bitcoin Cash served the needs of the first group, and Bitcoin SV served the needs of the second group.[4]

Each taxpayer holding Bitcoins prior to the hard fork was, in addition, granted an equal number of Bitcoin Cash. Effectively, a taxpayer now held two cryptoassets instead of one.[5]

---

[1] https://github.com/bitcoin/bips provides a list of BIP's and is the website through which new BIP's are submitted.
[2] https://medium.com/@galea/bitcoin-development-who-can-change-the-core-protocol-478b8ac5fe43.
[3] https://www.theverge.com/2018/4/12/17229796/bitcoin-cash-conflict-transactions-fight.
[4] https://en.wikipedia.org/wiki/Bitcoin_Cash.
[5] https://www.theverge.com/2018/4/12/17229796/bitcoin-cash-conflict-transactions-fight.

WHAT ARE THE TAX CONSEQUENCES OF THE 1 AUGUST 2017 'HARD FORK' IN BITCOIN?

11.3   The original cost of acquiring a Bitcoin should be allocated across the two cryptoassets arising out of the hard fork on a reasonable and proportionate basis, probably pro-rated according to the market value of each asset.[6] This cost is crucial to calculating the gain or profit when a Bitcoin is sold.

WHAT HAPPENS WHEN A NEW CRYPTOASSET IS NOT RECOGNISED BY THE EXCHANGE THROUGH WHICH A TAXPAYER HOLDS THEIR CRYPTOASSETS?

11.4   HMRC have recognised that after a hard fork, certain taxpayers may have a problem if they are holding their cryptoasset through an exchange that refuses to recognise the new asset.[7]

A case in point is Bitcoin Gold. Bitcoin Gold was created by a hard fork on 24 October 2017. It was subject to a 51% hashing attack in May 2018.[8] Due to concern about security vulnerabilities in the software, the exchange Bittrex delisted Bitcoin Gold.

HMRC have indicated that they will deal with these matters on a case by case basis. However, if the cryptoasset cannot be recovered then either:

(1)   all of the allowable cost of the original cryptoasset should be allocated to the cryptoasset that still remains; or

(2)   a negligible value claim should be made for the cryptoasset that cannot be recovered.

---

[6] *TCGA 1992, ss 43, 52(4)* in relation to cryptoassets held as an investment.
[7] Cryptoassets for individual, HMRC paper, 19 December 2018 – https://www.gov.uk/government/publications/tax-on-cryptoassets/cryptoassets-for-individuals.
[8] https://en.wikipedia.org/wiki/Bitcoin_Gold.

Chapter 12

Employment taxes

Focus

It is uncommon for employees in the UK to be paid in cryptocurrency. However, there is the possibility that this may change in the future.

Where a company pays an employee in cryptocurrency, they are obliged to withhold Pay As You Earn ('PAYE') and National Insurance Contributions ('NICs') on those payments where the cryptoasset is a 'readily convertible asset'. That is, where the cryptocurrency or cryptoasset could be sold on an orderly market for hard currency. Where an employer has the obligation to pay PAYE and NICs, there are two ways it could go about doing this:

1   they could pay the employee the net amount they are due, and pay the relevant PAYE and NICs to HMRC; or
2   the employee could pay the gross amount of their salary in cryptocurrency, and have the employee pay them back the PAYE and NICs that were due on that payment based on the market value of the cryptocurrency at the date it was due to be paid, within 90 days of the companies year end.

If an employee is paid in a cryptocurrency that is not a 'readily convertible asset', the employee has the obligation to pay PAYE and NICs in respect of the payments that they receive.

Cryptocurrency or cryptoassets received as remuneration for employment will be subject to income tax in the same way as salary received for employment.

An employee who later sells a cryptoasset will be subject to capital gains tax on that sale.

CRYPTOCURRENCY RECEIVED AS SALARY THAT IS A 'READILY CONVERTIBLE ASSET'

12.1   In the UK it is uncommon to pay an employee in cryptocurrency. A cryptocurrency exchange, Coin Corner that is registered in the Isle of Man, is one company that pays its employees in cryptocurrency.

Where an employer pays an employee in cryptocurrency, and that cryptocurrency is a 'readily convertible asset', that is, there exists, or is likely to exist, an orderly market where:

1   it can be realised for fiat currency directly; or
2   it can be realised for fiat currency indirectly, by trading it for another cryptoasset that could be converted into cryptocurrency;[1]

the employer will have the obligation to withhold PAYE and Class 1 NICs in respect of that payment.

PAYE and Class 1 NICs will have to be calculated based on the value that can be reasonably estimated for the cryptocurrency or cryptoasset at the date that it was due to be paid to the employee.[2] An employer is required to make these payments of PAYE and Class 1 NICs to HMRC, regardless of whether they are actually able to deduct them from the payment made to the employee.[3]

If the employer is unable to deduct all the PAYE and Class 1 NICs that are due on the employee's salary before the end of the employee's tax year, the employee must reimburse the employer for the 'due amount' of the PAYE and NICs that remain unpaid within 90 days of the end of the employer's tax year.

Where an employee does not reimburse an employer the 'due amount' within 90 days of the end of their tax year, this will be treated as income of the employee for which they are liable for income tax,[4] and the employer will be liable to make a further payment of PAYE and NICs based on the 'grossed up' amount of cryptocurrency salary that the employee received.

An employee disposing of this cryptocurrency at a later date will likely be liable for capital gains tax, as discussed above.

---

[1] *ITEPA 2003, s 702(1)(c), (2)*.
[2] *ITEPA 2003, s 696(1), (2)* in relation to PAYE.
[3] *ITEPA 2003, s 710(4)*.
[4] *ITEPA 2003, s 222(1)(c), (2)*.

CRYPTOCURRENCY RECEIVED AS SALARY THAT IS A *NOT* A 'READILY CONVERTIBLE ASSET'

12.2   Where an employee received cryptocurrency that is not a readily convertible asset, the employer does not have an obligation to withhold PAYE from payments of cryptocurrency made to the employee.

The employee will be liable for income tax on these payments.

The employer will be liable to deduct Class 1A NICs from these payments on the basis that they are 'payments in kind'.

Chapter 13

Non-domiciled individuals and inheritance tax

Focus

Non-domiciled individuals are subject to inheritance tax only on their UK assets, that is, assets that have a UK situs. The situs of cryptocurrency and cryptoassets is therefore of great importance for inheritance tax purposes.

I agree with the updated HMRC guidance released in December 2019 that cryptocurrency is most likely to have its situs in the jurisdiction where the person who holds that cryptocurrency is habitually resident. However, this may change going forward as the cryptocurrency markets become more sophisticated and potentially more regulated.

This means, at present, Bitcoin held by an individual/company habitually resident in the UK for the purposes of UK private international law will be a UK asset for inheritance purposes.

However, Bitcoin owned by an individual or company habitually resident in a jurisdiction outside the UK will be a non-UK asset.

In respect of other cryptoassets, the situs of each asset will have to be considered on a case by case basis. Tokenised land in which an individual or company has a direct interest will be situated wherever the land is based. The nature of the legal relationship in relation to other cryptoassets, and their situs, will have to be considered on a case by case basis.

It may be possible to structure arrangements to ensure that cryptocurrency/cryptoassets are non-UK assets.

It is probably wise to take advice in relation to whether a particular cryptoasset is a UK or non-UK asset and whether there are planning opportunities such that it could be classed as a non-UK asset.

13.1   *Inheritance Tax Act 1984 ('IHTA 1984'), s 1* states that inheritance tax is charged where there is a 'transfer of value' and that transfer is not an exempt transfer.

IHTA 1984, s 3 states:

> 'a transfer of value is a disposition made by a person (the transferor) as a result of which the value of his estate immediately after the disposition is less than it would be but for the disposition, and the amount by which it is less is the value transferred by the transfer.'

Authority on the meaning of 'disposition' is sparse.[1] The 1956 Privy Council case of *Ward v IRC*[2] offers the most authoritative guidance on the meaning of 'disposition'. In that case, the Privy Council was considering the meaning of the term 'disposition' in relation to the *Death Duties Act 1921 (NZ), s 39*. Lord Morton of Henryton, giving judgment for the court, agreed with Greeson J of the New Zealand Supreme Court that:

> 'the word 'disposition' is not a technical word but an ordinary English word of very wide meaning ....'[3]

The Oxford English dictionary defines 'disposition' to mean:

> 'the distribution or transfer of property to someone'.

It should be observed that all that *IHTA 1984, s 3* requires is a disposition by a taxpayer; it does not require that there be any disposition or transfer to someone else.[4]

There is no question that a transfer of cryptocurrency or a cryptoasset by an individual, where that cryptocurrency or cryptoasset has value, would be a 'disposition' that results in the value of their estate being lower than before the 'disposition' was made.

Therefore, the transfer of cryptocurrency or a cryptoasset would generally be a 'transfer of value' for the purposes of *IHTA 1984*. Therefore, where an individual makes a transfer of cryptocurrency to someone else either on death,[5] or within seven years of their death,[6] subject to an exemption applying, any such transfer will be subject to inheritance tax.

IS A DE-CENTRALISED CRYPTOCURRENCY 'PROPERTY' FOR THE PURPOSES OF *IHTA 1984, s 6(1)*?

13.2   Non-domiciled individuals are subject to UK inheritance tax only on their 'property' situated in the UK.[7]

---

[1] Aparna Nathan QC and Marika Lemos *McCutcheon on Inheritance Tax* (7th Edn, Sweet & Maxwell), paragraph 2-06.
[2] [1956] AC 391.
[3] *Ward v IRC* [1956] AC 391 at 400.
[4] Aparna Nathan QC and Marika Lemos *McCutcheon on Inheritance Tax* (7th Edn, Sweet & Maxwell), paragraph 2-06.
[5] *IHTA 1984, s 4*.
[6] *IHTA 1984, s 3A(4)*.
[7] *IHTA 1984, s 6(1)*.

For a non-domiciled UK taxpayer, the burning question is when is cryptocurrency or a cryptoasset 'property situated in the UK'[8] for the purposes of the *IHTA 1984?*'

IHTA 1984, s 272 states that 'property includes all rights and interests of any description but does not include a settlement power'.

Clearly, the definition of 'property' for inheritance tax purposes is extremely wide. However, there is no authoritative guidance on what is meant by the term 'property' for the purposes of *IHTA 1984, s 272*.

There are two possible arguments, both are somewhat ambitious. One is that a cryptocurrency like Bitcoin constitutes a new type of property at common law. The second is that as a matter of statutory interpretation, the term 'property' in *IHTA 1984, s 272* is very wide and should be impliedly interpreted along lines similar to the term 'property' in *TCGA 1992, s 21(1)* to include 'something that can be turned to account' (see **7.3**). This would include a cryptocurrency like Bitcoin.

Could Bitcoin be a new category of property at common law?

13.3   It should be observed that in the commercial law arena there is still heated debate as to precisely what rights, personal or proprietary, an individual has in respect of cryptocurrency. Lord Hodge recently observed that there was much doubt as to the nature of the property rights that someone acquires when they buy cryptocurrency and that a degree of international consensus would be needed if they are to be used more widely to facilitate cross-border commercial transactions.[9]

At common law, it is very unclear as to whether a de-centralised cryptocurrency like Bitcoin would be personal property. There is no UK authority directly on point. There are good arguments that a de-centralised cryptocurrency like Bitcoin could be personal property at common law, however, such an argument is challenging.

At common law, the position has long been there were only two categories of property, choses in action and choses in possession, and that there was no room for a third category.[10] Choses in

---

[8] Technically an asset is situated in either England and Wales, Scotland or Northern Ireland. In relation to cyrptocurrency/cryptoassets for most purposes it is unlikely to make a difference whether a particular cryptocurrency or cryptoasset is situated in England and Wales, Scotland or Northern Ireland and for simplicity, this publication simply discusses whether they are UK or non-UK assets.

[9] Financial Technology: Opportunities and Challenges to Law and Regulation, East China university of Political Science and Law, Shanghai, China, Lord Hodge, Justice of the Supreme Court of the United Kingdom, 26 October 2018, p 15.

[10] The authoritative basis for this is the dissenting judgment of Fry LJ in *Colonial Bank v Whinney* (1885) 30 Ch. D. 261 at 285 that was ultimately upheld by the House of Lords on appeal in *Colonial Bank v Whinney* (1886) 11 App Cas 426. The Court of Appeal in *Your Response Ltd v Datastream Business Media Ltd* [2014] EWCA Civ 281 rejected at invitation by the claimant to recognise a third category of property being intangible property (see particularly Moore-Bick LJ at [26] and Floyd LJ at [41]).

possession refer to tangible property that can be physically possessed. Choses in action are personal property rights that can only be claimed or enforced by taking legal action.[11] Based on the principles in *Your Response Ltd v Datastream Business Media Ltd*,[12] it would seem quite clear that decentralised cryptocurrencies like Bitcoin are neither choses in possession nor choses in action:

(i)   they are not choses in possession because they cannot be physically possessed; and

(ii) they are not choses in action because, unlike fiat currency, cryptocurrency does not give the holder a right of action against another party a right of action against another party. A holder of fiat currency, on the other hand, can compel another party to pay legal tender for the value of their currency.

In *Your Response Ltd v Datastream Business Media Ltd*, the Court of Appeal considered whether information on a database could be 'property' over which the claimant could maintain a possessory lien. Essentially, they held information on a database was not property such that a possessory lien could not be granted over the electronic information. Moore-Bick LJ at [26] with whom Davis LJ at [37] and Floyd LJ at [41] agreed, considered that it would be very difficult to accept that the common law recognises the existence of a third category of property, in addition to the current categories at common law, being a chose in possession and a chose in action.

Based on the decision in *Your Response Ltd v Datastream Business Media Ltd*, it would appear challenging to make the argument that a decentralised cryptocurrency like Bitcoin is a sui-generis form of personal property at common law.

However, it is interesting to note that in the recent case of *B2C2 Ltd v Quoine Pte Ltd*[13] involving abnormal trading in cryptocurrency in the Singapore International Commercial Court, Simon Thorley LJ was happy to conclude that cryptocurrency was personal property in a generic sense that could be held on trust.[14] He noted that the Defendant did not dispute that bitcoins were property. His reasoning was based on the classical statement of Lord Wilberforce in the House of Lords case of *National Provincial Bank v Ainsworth*[15] that, for a right of interest to be admitted to a new category of property:

> 'the right or interest must be definable, identifiable by third parties, capable in its nature of assumption by third parties, and have some degree of permanence or stability.'[16]

Simon Thorley LJ was content to recognise that Bitcoin was property in a generic sense without trying to categorise it as a chose in possession, a chose in action, or a hybrid category.

---

[11] See particularly the judgment of Moore-Bick LJ in *Your Response Ltd v Datastream Business Media Ltd* [2014] EWCA Civ 281 at [13].

[12] [2014] EWCA Civ 281.

[13] [2019] SGHC(I) 03.

[14] Ibid at [142].

[15] [1965] A.C. 1175.

[16] *National Provincial Bank v Ainsworth* [1965] A.C. 1175 at 1248.

In addition, recently in *Liam David Robertson v Persons Unknown*, a case concerning bitcoins that had been fraudulently stolen in a spearfishing attack and transferred to a third party, Mrs Justice Moulder granted an asset preservation order in relation to bitcoins held in a third party account of Coinbase UK Ltd, and considered that there was a serious issue to be tried in relation to whether Bitcoins were property. Mr Justice Jacobs continued the asset preservation order on the return date. This judgment has so far not been finalised or published.[17]

However, a compelling argument could be made to put the law of personal property on a more modern footing to account for technological developments. So much was acknowledged by Moore-Bick LJ in *Your Response Ltd v Datastream Business Media Ltd*[18] based on the minority decision in *OBG v Allan*.[19]

OBD v Allan was a Supreme Court case that considered whether the tort of conversion could be extended to provide a remedy where a receiver had taken control of the claimant's intangible contractual rights, after the receiver had been appointed under an invalid floating charge. The majority judgements considered that the tort of conversion applied only to tangible property.[20] However, the minority judgments of Lord Nicholls of Birkenhead and Lady Hale were prepared to extend the tort of conversion to cover intangible contractual rights, essentially because they considered that it was outmoded for the tort of conversion to only protect tangible property.[21]

Lady Hale espoused:

> 'The essential feature of property is that it has an existence independent of a particular person: it can be bought and sold, given and received, bequeathed and inherited, pledged or seized to secure debts, acquired (in the olden days) by a husband marrying its owner'.[22]

And further:

> 'Once the law recognises something as property, the law should extend a proprietary remedy to protect it'.[23]

---

[17] https://www.stewartslaw.com/news/cryptocurrency-bitcoin-asset-preservation-order-stewarts/.

[18] [2014] EWCA Civ 281 at [27].

[19] [2008] AC 1. The decision in *Armstrong DLW GmbH v Winnington Networks Ltd [2012] 3 All ER 425* also represents an interesting case where Judge Stephen Morris QC was prepared to find that a tradeable carbon emission allowance was property of a the claimant in the context of a proprietary restitution clam at common law by the claimant. Judge Morris QC was prepared to find that the allowances while the carbon emission allowances did not constitute chose in actions in the narrow sense that they could not be claimed or enforced at [61], they did constitute property in the wider sense whether they were a chose in action in the wider sense or intangible property. At [93], Judge Morris QC considered that there was greater scope to extend a proprietary remedy to the carbon emission allowances. That would be the case if he were considering the tort of conversion. Overall, Judge Morris QC was prepared to take an approach similar to the minority judgments in *OBG v Allan*.

[20] Lord Hoffmann at [106]Lord Walker of Gestingthorpe at [271],and Lord Brown of Eaton-Upon-Heywood at [321].

[21] See particularly [309]–[312] of the judgment of Lady Hale and [233]–[237] of the judgment of Lord Nicholls of Birkenhead at [233]–[237].

[22] OBG v Allan [2008] AC 1 at [309].

[23] Ibid, at [310].

In summary, Lady Hale appears open to recognising new forms of sui generis personal property. This approach is not dissimilar to the approach taken by Simon Thorley LJ in *B2C2 Ltd v Quoine Pte Ltd.*

In summary, if the issue of whether a decentralised cryptocurrency was personal property at common law came before the Supreme Court, the matter could potentially go either way, depending on the approach of the judges that sat on the case. However, on balance, making an argument that a decentralised cryptocurrency like Bitcoin is personal property does have challenges.

As a matter of statutory interpretation, the term 'property' in *IHTA 1984, s 272* would include a cryptocurrency like Bitcoin

13.4   It could also be argued that a cryptocurrency like Bitcoin should be 'property' for the purposes of *IHTA 1984, s 272* because, as a matter of statutory construction, a very broad interpretation of the term 'property' should be taken such that this it includes rights and interests that are not 'property' at common law. An argument for such an expansive view could be taken along the lines of the decision of the House of Lords in *O'Brien (Inspector of Taxes) Appellant v Benson's Hosiery (Holdings) Limited*[24] (see **7.1**) where the court took a purposive construction of the term 'asset', and impliedly 'property' for the purposes of what is now *TCGA 1992, ss 1(1)* and *21(1)*. Lord Russell of Killoween, giving judgment for the court, held that 'something that can be turned to account', regardless of whether it could be transferred or was assignable, was an 'asset' for the purposes of what is now *TCGA 1992, ss 1(1)* and *21(1)*. Impliedly, he also considered that 'something that could be turned to account' could also be considered 'property' for the purposes of *TCGA 1992, ss 1(1)* and *21(1)*.

Arguably, the scheme of IHTA 1984 allows for a very expansive view to be taken of the term 'property' for the purposes of *IHTA 1984, s 272*, such that it includes 'rights and interests' that may not be property at common law. There is no question that cryptocurrency constitutes a 'transfer of value' when it passes to a beneficiary on death, or is otherwise transferred within seven years of death. Taking a broad purposive construction of *IHTA 1984, s 6(1)*, it is reasonable to infer that it was the intention of the legislature to exempt a transfer of cryptocurrency where it is not situated in the UK on the basis that it constituted an 'interest of any description' for the purposes of *IHTA 1984, s 272* and therefore 'property' within *IHTA 1984, s 6(1) or 272*.

In sum, I agree with the updated HMRC guidance in December 2019 that cryptocurrency will constitute 'property' for the purposes of *IHTA 1984* on the basis that it is something that can be 'turned to account'.

---

[24] [1980] AC 562.

WHEN IS A DE-CENTRALISED CRYPTOCURRENCY LIKE BITCOIN SITUATED OUTSIDE THE UK?

13.5   As above, non-domiciled individuals are subject to UK inheritance tax only on their 'property' situated in the UK.[25]

Bitcoin is 'property' for the purposes of *IHTA 1984, s 6(1)* or *272*, the burning question then becomes, when is it situated in the UK for the purposes of *IHTA 1984*?

In relation to inheritance tax, the situs of an asset will be determined by reference to English private international law.[26] Every asset must be situated in a jurisdiction but can only ever be situated in one jurisdiction at any one time.[27]

The table below lists different intangible things and their situs for the purposes of UK private international law:

Intangible thing	Situs
Shares	Generally, the location of the share register[28]
Land	The jurisdiction where the land is situated[29]
Chattel	The jurisdiction where the chattel is physically located at any particular point in time[30]
Goodwill	In the jurisdiction where the business is located[31]

WHEN IS CRYPTOCURRENCY A UK ASSET OR A NON-UK ASSET?

13.6   The question then is, what are the appropriate connecting factor or factors for a de-centralised cryptocurrency to determine where it is situated?

There is no really good answer to this question. There is no particular precedent that gives a nice neat answer. Essentially, it is necessary to resort to first principles. The nature of determining the situs of an intangible asset means that there will be an element of arbitrariness in determining the touchstone for the situs of cryptocurrency.

---

[25] *IHTA 1984, s 6(1)*.
[26] *New York Life Insurance Company v Public Trustee* [1924] 2 Ch 101 Warrington LJ at 117.
[27] *R v Williams* [1942] AC 541 at 559.
[28] *Att-Gen v Higgins* (1857) 2 H&N 339.
[29] *Phillipson-Stow v IRC* [1961] AC 727 Viscount Simonds impliedly at 744 and Lord Denning impliedly at 762.
[30] *Air Foyle and Another v Capital Centre Ltd* [2002] EWHC 2535 (Comm) at [42] citing *Cammell v Sewell* (1860) 5 H&N 728.
[31] *IRC v Muller & Co's Margarine Ltd* [1901] AC 217 per Lord James of Hereford at 234. And Lord Lindley at 235.

The best answer comes from Professor Andrew Dickinson at the University of Oxford. He argues that a de-centralised cryptocurrency is situated where the participant who controls it resides or carries on business. If a person resides or carries on business in more than one jurisdiction, then the cryptocurrency that person controls should be located in the jurisdiction with which that person is most closely connected.[32] Professor Dickinson adopts the view that cryptocurrency should be situated where the individual that controls it resides because it is an intangible asset in the same way that goodwill is an intangible asset. Goodwill is situated where the business it relates to is carried on.[33] If it were the goodwill of a sole trader, goodwill would be located wherever the sole trader carried on their business.[34]

Residence is arguably a suitable touchstone, at least partially because it has an element of permanence. Residence is also suitable because crypto currency attaches to a person. Arguably, in the context of considering where a cryptocurrency like Bitcoin is situated for the purposes of *IHTA 1984, s 6(1)* or *272*, residence refers to the English private international law concept of residence being 'habitual residence'.[35]

Another possibility is to use the 'domicile' of an individual as being where cryptocurrency that they control is situated. Domicile is generally preferred to habitual residence in English private international law.[36] However, domicile isn't quite as appropriate in the case of a cryptocurrency like Bitcoin. An individual can be resident in one jurisdiction for many years, spend most of that time in that jurisdiction, but have a domicile in a completely different jurisdiction. Adopting domicile as to the touchstone for situs of a cryptocurrency does not fit easily with the analogy that, like goodwill, it attaches to the individual. If domicile were the touchstone, cryptocurrency could be situated in a jurisdiction even though the individual controlling it was barely in that jurisdiction, if at all, during the time that they controlled the cryptocurrency.

Another possibility could be that the jurisdiction where the individual holds their private key could be the local situation for the cryptocurrency or cryptoassets connected with that private key. The touchstone of a private key to determine the local situation of cryptocurrency or cryptoassets has some appeal because an individual uses their key to sign/initiate transfers of cryptocurrency or cryptoassets, and this is how they ultimately control their cryptocurrency or cryptoassets. However, a private key can be stored in multiple locations.[37] For instance, one private key could be stored on an individual's local computer or phone, while another is stored at a crypto exchange in another jurisdiction. Also, it is possible to split a private key into several pieces and store these

---

[32] Fox & Green (ed) *Cryptocurrencies in Public and Private Law* (OUP, 2019)at para 5.109.

[33] *Dicey, Morris and Collins on the Conflict of Laws* (15th Edn, Sweet & Maxwell), at para 22-050, referring to *IRC v Muller & Co's Margarine Ltd AC 217* Lord Lindley at 235.

[34] The nature of a sole trader business usually means that most sole traders would have very little if any goodwill, however, the point of principle still stands.

[35] See in particular *Dicey, Morris and Collins on the Conflict of Laws* (15th Edn, Sweet & Maxwell), at paras 6–118 onwards.

[36] *Dicey, Morris and Collins on the Conflict of Laws* (15th Edn, Sweet & Maxwell), at para 6–172.

[37] Narayanan, Bonneau, Felten, Miller and Goldfeder *Bitcoin and Cryptocurrency Technologies: A comprehensive introduction* (Princeton University Press, 2016), p 84.

pieces in multiple locations/jurisdictions.[38] In fact, this is encouraged because it increases security and avoids having a single point of failure where a private key held in one location could be hacked or lost.[39] Given these issues, a private key is an unsuitable touchstone to determine the local situation of cryptocurrency or cryptoassets.

In sum, any rule for determining the local situation of intangible property will be somewhat arbitrary. I agree with the updated HMRC guidance released in December 2019 that the jurisdiction where the person is habitually resident or conducts their business is likely to be the most suitable touchstone for determining the local situation of cryptocurrency. If the person has more residences or conducts business in more than one jurisdiction, then their cryptocurrency should be situated in whichever jurisdiction they are more closely connected with.

The situs of any particular cryptocurrency may change going forward, particularly if cryptocurrency goes more mainstream and becomes more regulated.

WHEN ARE OTHER CRYPTOASSETS UK ASSETS OR NON-UK ASSETS?

13.7 The rights that an investor acquires in many initial coin offering are opaque. Determining the legal rights that a crypto asset creates is a question of fact and circumstance in each case. The Whitepaper will typically be the best starting point, although it may not make clear what legal relationships are created between an investor and issuer. It may be necessary to examine other documentation and representations being made in relation to a particular cryptoasset. Each case will turn on its own facts.

The person or investor is given an interest in the underlying asset

13.8 'Tokenisation' of an asset refers to the process by which a Blockchain-based token is issued to represent an interest in an asset. These tokens are often referred to as 'security tokens' and can also be classified as an 'asset token' as outlined at **2.1**. Tokenisation of an asset enables greater liquidity in markets for assets such as fine art. These assets can be divided into relatively small interests represented by security tokens and then traded on exchanges.

Tokenisation of assets is happening on a small scale at present. For instance, 49% of Andy Warhol's painting, '14 small electric chairs', was tokenised.[40] There are also initial coin offerings that tokenise real estate.

---

[38] Ibid.
[39] Ibid.
[40] https://www.ccn.com/andy-warhols-multi-million-dollar-painting-tokenized-and-sold-on-blockchain/.

Where an investor obtains a direct interest in the underlying property of the initial coin offering, it will be the situs rule for that underlying asset that determines whether it is UK-situated or situated outside the UK. Real estate will be situated in the jurisdiction that it is located.[41] A fine art painting is a chattel and is situated in the jurisdiction it is physically located at a particular point in time.[42]

The person or investor has a right to income

13.9 Asset tokens may grant an investor an equity or debt like interest (see **2.1**). The nature of this interest will need to be characterised in each case.

If the relationship the asset token creates can be described as creating a debtor/creditor relationship between the investor and a particular person, the investor asset is likely to be situated in the jurisdiction of the issuer.[43]

It may be that the 'asset token' creates an equity-like interest and a contractual relationship between the investor and a person issuing the token. If this is the case, the situs of the investor's interest will be the jurisdiction where the legal obligation can be enforced.[44]

A POTENTIAL WAY TO RESOLVE THE AMBIGUITY AND HAVE CRYPTOCURRENCY/CRYPTOASSETS CLASSIFIED AS A NON-UK ASSET

13.10 There is a tremendous amount of ambiguity in relation to whether cryptocurrency or cryptoassets are situated in the UK or outside the UK for inheritance tax purposes.

A potential solution is to structure the ownership of cryptocurrency, and possibly cryptoassets, through an offshore company or trust. However, there will be a tax charge getting the asset out of the UK and the use of an offshore fund raises many other tax issues.

It would probably be wise to take advice in relation to the situs of a cryptoasset and whether some planning can be undertaken to ensure that asset is a non-UK asset for inheritance tax purposes.

---

[41] *Phillipson-Stow v IRC* [1961] AC 727 Viscount Simonds impliedly at 744 and Lord Denning impliedly at 762.
[42] *Air Foyle and Another v Capital Centre Ltd* [2002] EWHC 2535 (Comm) at [42] citing *Cammell v Sewell* (1860) 5 H&N 728.
[43] *New York Life Insurance Company v Public Trustee* [1924] 2 Ch 101 Pollock MR at 107 and 108, Warrington LJ at 114, per Atkin LJ at 119.
[44] *Sutherland v Administrator of German Property* [1934] 1 KB 423 (CA), per Scrutton LJ at 432, Lawrence LJ at 433 and Greer LJ at 434.

Chapter 14

Non-domiciled individuals and capital gains tax

Focus

I agree with updated guidance from HMRC released in December 2019 that cryptocurrency should be both an 'asset' and 'property' for the purposes of *TCGA 1992, s 275A(2)*.

The updated HMRC guidance in December 2019 considers that cryptocurrency is a UK asset for purposes of a non-domiciled individual who uses the remittance basis for capital gains tax purposes. Impliedly, this is on the basis that *TCGA 1992, ss 275, 275A* and *275B* do not constitute a 'code' that prescribes the location of an asset for the purposes of the TCGA 1992. HMRC considers that no part of *TCGA 1992, ss 275* and *275A* applies to determine the location of cryptocurrency that an individual holds, and therefore it must be the residence of the taxpayer who holds that cryptocurrency that determines its location for the purposes of *TCGA 1992*. That is, the cryptocurrency of a UK resident taxpayer will be a UK asset for the purposes of *TCGA 1992*.

There is a counterargument to this. That is that *TCGA 1992, s 275*, in conjunction with *ss 275A* and *275B*, constitutes a 'code' for the purpose of determining the location of all assets for capital gains tax purposes. Based on this argument, in many cases, a cryptocurrency like Bitcoin could be argued to be a non-UK asset. On this argument, a cryptocurrency like Bitcoin will be created where it is first 'mined'. Anecdotally, most 'mining' activities take place outside the UK, and a relatively small proportion of activities take place in the UK. As in **Chapter 13**, there is a good argument that cryptocurrency is analogous to goodwill in the sense that it is an intangible asset that attaches to an individual personally and that it should be treated as situated where that individual is habitually resident. If this is the case, and a Bitcoin is 'mined' and first created by a party who is habitually resident in a foreign jurisdiction, it is hard to conceive how UK law could apply to such an asset.

Based on this counter-argument, it should be observed that there is also a possible argument UK law could apply on the basis the participants on the Bitcoin network have contractual obligations towards each other, or obligations 'akin to a contract' towards each other. This then raises a complex question of whether it should be the law of England and Wales or the law of a foreign jurisdiction that should apply to determine the rights of the participants in relation to the creation of a cryptocurrency token. Each case turns on its own circumstances. However, there is likely to be a good argument that the laws of a foreign jurisdiction apply under Article 4 of Rome I in the case of Bitcoin. If that is the case, the Bitcoin will be a non-UK asset for the purposes of the non-domiciliary CGT regime.

There is a practical difficulty in relation to proof of where a Bitcoin was first created. It is possible to trace through the Blockchain and identify the public address of the party who 'mined' a Bitcoin. It may be possible to uncover the identity of the party and jurisdiction where they were resident when they first 'mined' the Bitcoin. However, in many cases, this is likely not to be possible. This practical difficulty is something likely to be raised by HMRC – that this counter-argument in itself is not reasonable, and for this reason, Parliament could not have intended that *TCGA 1992, ss 275, 275A* and *275B* constitute a code.

A non-domiciled taxpayer who files a return claiming that they are entitled to the non-domiciliary CGT regime in relation to Bitcoin or another cryptocurrency therefore takes a risk and is likely to be challenged by HMRC.

A possible way around these problems is to hold cryptocurrency through an offshore company or trust. However, care needs to be taken implementing these structures as they raise many other tax issues.

Whether a non-domiciled taxpayer can classify other cryptocurrency or cryptoassets as non-UK assets for the purposes of the non-domiciliary regime is a matter that would have to be considered on a case by case basis. The analysis may well differ from Bitcoin.

CRYPTOCURRENCY – APPLICATION OF THE NON-DOMICILED CGT REGIME

14.1   As above at **7.1**, there is no question that cryptocurrency is an 'asset' for the purposes of *TCGA 1992, ss 1(1)* and *21(1)*, and are also impliedly 'property' for the purposes of those sections.

In relation to a non-domiciled individual, it is relevant to determine the situs of cryptocurrency for the purposes of *TCGA 1992*.

TCGA 1992 provides statutory situs rules to determine the situs of assets.

TCGA 1992, s 275 lists a number of assets (eg shares, debts, patents etc) and states their situs. Cryptocurrency does not fall into any of these categories.

TCGA 1992, s 275A provides that a CGT statutory situs rule for 'intangible assets' whose situs *TCGA 1992* does not otherwise make provision for.[1]

---

[1] *TCGA 1992, ss 275A, 275B(1).*

TCGA 1992, s 275A (2) states that 'intangible asset' means:

(a) Intangible or incorporeal property and includes a thing in action; or

(b) Anything under the law of a foreign country that corresponds to or is similar to intangible or incorporeal property or a thing in action.

As above at **7.1**, there is no question that cryptocurrency will be an 'asset' for the purposes of *TCGA 1992* based on the decision in *O'Brien (Inspector of Taxes) v Benson's Hosiery (Holdings) Ltd.*[2] Impliedly, from the principles in the decision in *O'Brien*, cryptocurrency would also impliedly be 'property' for the purposes of *TCGA 1992*.

Based on the decision in *O'Brien (Inspector of Taxes) v Benson's Hosiery (Holdings) Ltd*, there is no question that cryptocurrency could be described as an 'intangible asset' for the purposes of *TCGA 1992, s 275A (2)*. Based on the principles in *O'Brien*, cryptocurrency is also impliedly 'property' for the purposes of *TCGA 1992*, even though it may not be property at common law. There is nothing in the scheme of the legislation requiring either the word 'asset' or 'property' to be interpreted in a more restrictive way than the main charging provisions (*TCGA 1992, ss 1(1), 21(1)*).[3] It would be a strange result if an individual could be subject to capital gains tax on the gains they realise from the sale of cryptocurrency, but could not be able to utilise the benefits of the non-domiciliary regime for capital gains tax.

In sum, cryptocurrency should be considered both an 'intangible asset' and 'intangible property' for the purposes of *TCGA 1992, s 275A (2)*. It will be *TCGA 1992, s 275A (2)* that applies to determine the location of cryptocurrency, because, as above, cryptocurrency does not fall into any of the categories of assets whose situs is prescribed by *TCGA 1992, s 275*. I have a different view from the updated guidance released by HMRC in December 2019 in this regard.

HMRC'S VIEW THAT CRYPTOCURRENCY IS UK-SITUATED FOR THE PURPOSES OF *TCGA 1992*

14.2 Although it is not explicitly stated, in HMRC's view, *TCGA 1992, ss 275, 275A* and *275B* do not constitute a 'code' for the purposes of determining the location of all assets for the purposes of *TCGA 1992*. On this basis, they consider that no particular section in *TCGA 1992, ss 275* and *275A* prescribes the location of cryptocurrency, and therefore it must be the residency of the holder of cryptocurrency that determines its location for the purposes of *TCGA 1992*.

---

[2] [1980] AC 562.
[3] It should also be noted that the explanatory memorandum to *Finance (No 2) Bill 2005* that introduced section *TCGA 1992, 275A(2)* consistently refers to 'intangible assets' rather than the possibly more restrictive term 'intangible property' see particularly clause 34, Schedule 4 paragraphs 30 and 31 to the explanatory memorandum of clause 34 of *Finance (No 2) Bill 2005*.

The counter argument to this is that *TCGA 1992, s 275*, in conjunction with *ss 275A* and *275B*, constitutes a 'code' for the purposes of determining the location of all assets for the purposes of *TCGA 1992*. Paragraph 30 of the explanatory memorandum to *Finance Bill 2005*, that introduced *TCGA 1992, ss 275A* and *275B*, suggests that Parliament intended that *TCGA 1992, s 275A*, in particular, was to constitute a 'code' for determining the location of an intangible asset whose location is not otherwise determined by *TCGA 1992*. The counter-argument would be that a purposive reading of *TCGA 1992, ss 275A* and *275B* achieves this.

Based on this counter-argument, cryptocurrency is 'intangible property' pursuant to *TCGA 1992, s 275A(2)* and it will be intangible property whose location is not otherwise determined, as specified in *TCGA 1992, s 275 (1)* because *TCGA 1992, s 275* does not make provision for determining the location of this asset. Based on this counter-argument, cryptocurrency will be deemed to have a UK situs where, at the time that the asset was created, any right of interest that comprises the asset was:

(a)   governed by, or otherwise subject to, or;

(b)   enforceable under;

any part of the law of the UK.[4]

Based on this counter argument, if *TCGA 1992, ss 275A(3)* and *275B(2)* do not deem an asset to have a UK situs, and nothing else in *TCGA 1992, ss 275A* and *275B* deems the asset to have a UK situs, then the asset concerned must have a non-UK situs because *TCGA 1992, ss 275, 275A* and *275B* constitutes a 'code' for determining the situs of all assets for the purposes of *TCGA 1992*.

IF *TCGA 1992, ss 275A* AND *275B* CONSTITUTE A 'CODE' FOR DETERMINING THE LOCATION OF AN ASSET FOR THE PURPOSES OF *TCGA 1992*, WHEN DOES CRYPTOCURRENCY HAVE A UK SITUS?

14.3   There has never been a decided case on what is meant by whether UK law applies to a right or interest comprising the asset.

Arguably, a law of any part of the UK could potentially apply to an asset or thing overseas where it had extraterritorial application. Arguably, in a case where there was a conflict between UK law and the law of a foreign jurisdiction, it would then be a question for UK private international law, assuming an action was or could be undertaken in the UK, as to whether a law of any part of the UK applied to that asset at the time that it was created.

---

[4] *TCGA 1992, ss 275A(3), 275B (2).*

Whether any part of the law of the UK applies at the time that any particular cryptocurrency is created is potentially a very difficult question. Every case turns on its own circumstances.

Bitcoin would generally be taken to be created when it is first 'mined' by a miner node. 'Mining pools' currently dominate mining activity. Very broadly, a 'mining pool' is an arrangement where miners 'club together' and share the risks and rewards of mining. The pool is generally organised by a pool manager who receives a fee from the other miners for performing this activity.

Presently, Bitcoin miner nodes appear to be basing themselves in jurisdictions where energy costs to power their computer equipment are low. Typically, these are jurisdictions outside the UK. More than 70% of miner nodes are estimated to be in China because China is a country that has very low electricity costs.[5]

At first blush, it is difficult to conceive of UK law applying to the act of 'mining' or creating bitcoin in another jurisdiction.

It is possible to argue that UK law could apply on the basis that there are contractual obligations between all parties who join the Bitcoin network, possibly similar to an unincorporated association. However, there is nothing explicit in the license agreement for Bitcoin Core or any other documentation that makes it explicit that participants on the network have a contractual relationship with anyone else on the network. Bitcoin has no formal structure. In summary, there is some doubt as to whether the participants on the Bitcoin network have contractual obligations towards one another under UK law.

IS THERE A 'CONTRACT' PURSUANT TO REGULATION (EC) NO 593/2008 OF THE EUROPEAN PARLIAMENT AND OF THE COUNCIL OF 17 JUNE 2008 ON THE LAW APPLICABLE TO CONTRACTUAL OBLIGATIONS (ROME 1)

14.4   Rome I is the EU regulation that provides for determining the applicable law in relation to a contractual obligation in the UK from 17 December 2009.

Article 1(1) of Rome 1 states that the regulation applies to 'contractual obligations in civil and commercial matters'. However, as stated above, there is some doubt as to whether the participants of the Bitcoin network have contractual obligations towards one another. The question then arises, could participants operating on the Bitcoin network fall within Rome 1.

---

[5] https://www.buybitcoinworldwide.com/mining/pools/.

Professor Andrew Dickinson has set out an extensive and well-reasoned argument for why the participants in the Bitcoin network could be characterised as 'contractual' within the European Private International Law instruments, and particularly Rome I, even if the relationships that the parties have don't quite to contractual obligations for the purposes of national law.[6] Professor Dickinson points out that the parties relationship on the Bitcoin network could be described as being a 'matter related to contract' within the Brussels I regime for jurisdiction purposes on the basis that the European Court had held that obligations that existed between members of an unincorporated association were a 'matter relating to a contract'.[7] Further, he argues that the relationship between participants on the Bitcoin network could be described as being 'a matter relating to contract' based on *Case C-27/02, Engler v Janus Versand GmbH*.[8] In that case, it was held that a statutory obligation to pay a prize offered as an incentive to conclude a contract for the sale of goods fell within the description of a 'matter relating to a contract' even where a prize was paid out, and no contract had been concluded with the consumer.[9] In essence, Professor Dickinson makes a compelling argument that the relationship of the participants on the Bitcoin network said to be 'sufficiently akin to that between parties that is indisputably contractual' such that a common set of rules should identify a court of competent jurisdiction to resolve disputes between them,[10] and also the existence and extent of participants contractual obligations towards one another, including the choice of law the, should apply to those obligations.[11] It will be Rome 1 that determines these latter matters.

APPLICATION OF ROME 1 TO THE CREATION OF BITCOINS

14.5   The following analysis proceeds on the basis that a party is able to bring the relationships between the participants on the Bitcoin network within Rome 1. As previously stated, there is no formal documentation that governs the relationships of participants on the Bitcoin network, let alone which specifies which law should apply in the event of a dispute.

It is therefore relevant to refer to Article 4 of Rome 1 that provides for the 'Applicable law in the absence of choice'.

In interpreting the articles of Rome I, the courts should arguably take a broad purposive approach to interpretation, and not an approach that is constrained in a narrow literal way or otherwise constrained by national rules of construction.[12]

---

[6] *Cryptocurrencies in Public Law and Private Law*, edited by David Fox and Sarah Green, see particularly paras 5.29–5.31.

[7] Ibid, at para 5.29.

[8] [2005] ECR I-481 at paras 45–59. *Cryptocurrencies in Public Law and Private Law* (above) at para 5.30.

[9] Ibid. at para 5.31.

[10] Those rules being the *Brussels Regime*.

[11] *Cryptocurrencies in Public Law and Private Law* (above), at para 5.31.

[12] *Iran Continental Shelf Oil Company and others v IRI International Corporation* [2002] EWCA Civ 1024 per Clarke LJ at [13]–[15] (with Carnwarth LJ at [93] and Ward LJ at [95] agreeing) took this approach in relation to Article 18 of the Rome Convention, which is the predecessor to recital 16 of Rome I. The wording of recital 16 of Rome 1 is different from Article 18 of the Rome Convention but arguably embodies the same spirit of interpretation.

Article 4(1) of Rome I provides for how the applicable law should be determined for a number of different types of contracts. However, none of these types of contracts would apply to a participant on the Bitcoin network.

Articles 4(2), 4(3) and 4(4) of Rome I provides as follows:

'(2) Where the contract is not covered by paragraph 1 or where the elements of the contract would be covered by more than one of points (a) to (h) of paragraph 1, the contract shall be governed by the law of the country where the party required to effect characteristic performance of the contract has his habitual residence.'

'(3) Where it is clear from all the circumstances of the case that the contract is manifestly more closely connected with a country other than that indicated in paragraphs 1 and 2, the law of that other country shall apply.'

'(4) Where the law applicable cannot be determined pursuant to paragraphs 1 and 2, the contract shall be governed by the law of the country with which it is most closely connected.'

Article 4(2) – identification of the party who effects characteristic performance of the contract

14.6   First, it is necessary to consider Article 4(2). In relation to the 'mining' or creation of a Bitcoin, is it possible to identify the party who effects characteristic performance of the contract.

There is little guidance in case law that is relevant to Bitcoin as to what is meant by 'characteristic performance'.

Dicey's Conflict of Laws (15th Edn) provides the following commentary on 'characteristic performance':

'The object of the doctrine of characteristic performance is to isolate the obligation incumbent on one of the parties which is peculiar to the type of contract in issue, or which marks the nature of the contract, and thereby link the contract to the social and economic environment of which it will form a part.'[13]

In relation to the activity of creating a Bitcoin, clearly, the activity of 'mining' involves the most computer power and takes up the most energy and hard work. Verification of the 'proof of work' produced by a 'miner' is a relatively straight forward and quick process.[14] Arguably, it is the 'mining' activity that produces a 'proof of work' that marks the nature of any relationship or contract. Therefore, it is the habitual residence of the party that undertakes the 'mining' activity

---

[13] *Dicey, Morris and Collins on the Conflict of Laws* 15th Edition, Albert Dicey, at paragraph 32-077.
[14] Bank of England Quarterly Bulletin 2014 Q 3, Vol 54 No. 3 262 at p 269.

that produces a new Bitcoin that determines which applicable law will apply. As above, in the overwhelming majority of cases, a 'miner' will be outside the UK. Therefore, it would most likely be the law of a foreign country that would apply to any contractual obligation in the creation of a Bitcoin under Article 4(2).

This legal issue also raises a potentially difficult factual issue for both the taxpayer and HMRC. In the case of a de-centralised currency like Bitcoin, it is possible to trace a single piece of cryptocurrency back to the public address of the person or entity that 'mined' or created it.[15] Bitcoin is pseudo-anonymous, in the sense that users can only be identified on the network by their public address, essentially an account number.[16] However, a user's identity may be revealed by in several different ways, including by interacting with their bank or paying another party with Bitcoin or trading on a cryptocurrency exchange.[17] Therefore, it is possible for either a taxpayer or HMRC to discover the identity of the party who 'mined' a Bitcoin and potentially in which jurisdiction they were located. HMRC has the added advantage that it could use its 'exchange of information' powers in a double tax treaty to obtain further information. Whether this was possible would be a matter of fact and circumstance in every case. It is a matter of speculation whether it would be possible to demonstrate in which jurisdiction a 'miner' was resident when they first 'mined' or created a Bitcoin. Realistically, most taxpayers would probably not undertake this exercise. Realistically, HMRC could try and uncover the identity and jurisdiction of a party who 'mined' Bitcoin in at least some cases.

The taxpayer generally bears the burden of positively proving that an assessment is incorrect and what the correct amount of the assessment should have been. However, HMRC must generally first offer at least some evidence of the matters in dispute to cast the burden of proof on the taxpayer. It is a matter of speculation whether they will be able to do this in any particular case. In many cases, it may not be possible. This difficulty is something that would be used by HMRC to argue that a statutory construction of *TCGA 1992, ss 275, 275A* and *275B* that these provisions constituted a code for determining the location of an asset for the purposes of *TCGA 1992* is something that Parliament could never have intended.

Interaction of Article 4(2) with Article 4(3) and (4) of Rome I

14.7 A court may take the view that it was not possible to determine the habitual residence of a party who effected characteristic performance of their obligations by 'mining' Bitcoin because of the pseudo-anonymous nature of Bitcoin.

---

[15] Technology and Governance, Rainer Böhme, Nicolas Christin, Benjamin Edelman, and Tyler Moore, Journal of Economic Perspectives, Volume 29, Number 2, Spring 2015 213 at 215.

[16] Ibid. at p217.

[17] Ibid. at 229 and https://99bitcoins.com/know-more-top-seven-ways-your-identity-can-be-linked-to-your-bitcoin-address/.

This means it is necessary to consider Article 4(3) and Article 4(4) of Rome I.

Article 4(3) of Rome I will only displace the presumption in Article 4(2) of Rome I where it can clearly be shown that it is connected with another country.[18] In the case of Bitcoin, there are validators all over the world. It is very difficult to see how anyone could use Article 4(3) to argue that the creation of a Bitcoin is connected with some country other than where the 'miner' is habitually resident.

This leaves Article 4(4) of Rome I. If a court considered that it was not possible to determine under Article 4(2) of Rome I either:

(1) 'characteristic performance' in relation to obligations that lead to the creation of a Bitcoin; or
(2) the 'habitual residence' of the party who effected characteristic performance of the creation of a Bitcoin because of the pseudo-anonymous nature of Bitcoin;

it would be necessary to refer to Article 4(4) of Rome I that states that the 'contract will be governed by the country with which it is most closely connected'. Arguably, the performance of obligations in relation to 'mining' should be connected with the country where the 'miner' performs those obligations. As above, most mining pools are located outside the UK. There is, therefore, a strong possibility that the laws of a foreign jurisdiction may apply to a bitcoin when it is first created. However, this all depends on the particular jurisdiction. There is also the possibility that the laws of a foreign jurisdiction do not apply at all. If this were the case, UK law could potentially apply to cryptocurrency when it was first created.

BREXIT – REVERSION TO THE COMMON LAW

14.8 It is not entirely clear whether the UK will continue to apply Rome I after Brexit. It could apply a modified instrument. It could also revert to the common law position.

The case of *Amin Rasheed Shipping Corp v Kuwait Insurance*[19] is the leading common law UK private international law authority on choosing the applicable law where a contract is silent as to which law applies. Lord Diplock espoused that it is the 'proper law' that the parties intended apply to the contract, and it is inferred from the terms of the contract and all the surrounding circumstances.[20] Lord Diplock also accepted that the determination of the 'proper law' could

---

[18] *Ennstone Building Products Ltd v Stanger Ltd* [2002] EWCA Civ 916 per Keene LJ at [41] with Potter LJ at [52] agreeing. In that case, Keene LJ was considering Article 4(2) and 4(4) of the Rome Convention, which is similar to Article 4(2) and 4(3) of Rome I.
[19] [1984] AC 50.
[20] *Amin Rasheed Shipping Corp v Kuwait Insurance* [1984] AC 50, per Lord Diplock at 60, 61.

be stated to be 'with which system of law does the transaction have its closest and most real connection.'[21]

Realistically, an analysis under common law as to what the applicable law should be in relation to parties performing obligations to create Bitcoin would likely follow a similar analysis to that undertaken above in relation to Rome I.

CONCLUSION

14.9   A non-domiciled taxpayer who files a return claiming the remittance basis for CGT purposes in relation to their Bitcoin transactions will often have an arguable position that their Bitcoin is a non-UK asset. However, a taxpayer filing on this basis takes a risk, and it is a position that is likely to be challenged by HMRC.

The safest course is to hold Bitcoins/cryptocurrency through a properly structured offshore company or trust. In this way, the taxpayer gets certainty that they are holding a non-UK asset and that they can use the non-domiciliary regime for the purposes of the cryptocurrency transactions that they enter in to.

The analysis may be different for other cryptocurrencies. Whether there is a defensible position that a particular cryptocurrency will be a UK or non-UK situate asset for CGT purpose will depend on the facts of each case. It would be sensible to seek advice in relation to these matters.

OTHER CRYPTOASSETS – APPLICATION OF THE NON-DOMICILED CGT REGIME

14.10   Where a cryptoasset is situated in a non-UK asset for the purposes of the non-domiciliary CGT regime is a matter of fact and circumstance in each case. In some cases, the ownership rights that cryptoassets, and whether they are a UK asset or a non-UK asset may be particularly complicated.

The starting point will be *TCGA 1992, s 275* that contains statutory situs rules for the purposes of CGT.

---

[21] Ibid, at 61.

Interest in land granted

14.11   By way of example, where land or property has been 'tokenised', and that land or property is a foreign jurisdiction, that land or property will be deemed to be situated in a foreign jurisdiction[22] and will, therefore, be a non-UK asset for the purposes of the non-domiciliary CGT regime.

Cryptoasset creating a debtor-creditor relationship

14.12   If the cryptoasset creates a debtor-creditor relationship between a UK tax resident investor and the issuer, the UK tax resident will be a creditor and that asset will be deemed to be a UK asset for the purposes of the non-domiciliary CGT regime.[23]

Cryptoasset creating an equity-like return

14.13   A cryptoasset that offered an equity-like return would most likely have its situs determined under *TCGA 1992, s 275A*. A potentially complicated analysis as to whether a law of any part of the UK applied to that asset when it was created would have to be made as would have to be done with cryptocurrency. Each case would turn on its own facts and circumstances.

---

[22] *TCGA 1992, s 275(1)(a).*
[23] *TCGA 1992, s 275(1)(c).*

Chapter 15

Value Added Tax ('VAT')

Focus

VAT is generally payable on goods and services purchased with cryptocurrency in the normal way.

However, where cryptocurrency is used as a form of payment, the supply of cryptocurrency itself will be exempt from VAT.

Income received from mining activities will be exempt from VAT.

The issue of utility tokens/voucher in an ICO is particularly complicated from a VAT point of view. They may constitute a 'single purpose' voucher on which VAT is payable upon issue and transfer. However, they may also constitute a 'multi-purpose' voucher on which VAT will be payable upon redemption. They may also potentially constitute a prepayment for goods or services.

Each case will depend on its own circumstances and advice should be sought as appropriate.

INTRODUCTION

15.1   There is no question that a good or service purchased with cryptocurrency or in exchange for a crypto asset is subject to VAT treatment in the normal way. VAT will be calculated on the sterling value of the cryptocurrency at the time that good or service is supplied.[1]

However, there is an interesting question as to whether the supply of cryptocurrency or a cryptoasset itself constitutes the supply of a service[2] on which VAT should be charged.

---

[1] Revenue and Customs Brief 9 (2014): Bitcoin and other cryptocurrencies, 3 March 2014, VAT treatment of Bitcoin and similar currencies.
[2] *VATA 1994, s 5(3)* in conjunction with *VATA 1994, Sch 4.*

CRYPTOCURRENCY/CRYPTOASSETS USED AS A FORM OF PAYMENT

15.2   HMRC accept that where cryptocurrency is converted to a fiat currency, be it Sterling or otherwise, no VAT will be due on the value of the cryptocurrency.[3]

HMRC consider that income received for arranging or carrying out services in Bitcoin/cryptocurrency is exempt from VAT pursuant to Article 135(1)(d) of the VAT Directive.[4]

The ECJ has also considered this matter in the case of *Skatteverket v David Hedqvist*.[5] This case was a referral from the Supreme Administrative Court in Sweden. The taxpayer was Mr David Hedqvist. He desired to carry on a business through a website, where he would buy and sell cryptocurrency from private individuals and companies and also buy and sell this cryptocurrency on exchanges or hold some of it for investment. In this case, Mr Hedqvist did not propose to charge a fee. He instead proposed to make a profit on trading a spread on the cryptocurrency that he would be buying and selling.

The Supreme Administrative Court in Sweden referred two questions to the ECJ for a preliminary ruling:

(1)   Do the transactions that Mr Hedqvist proposes to enter in to constitute the supply of a services for consideration pursuant to Article 2(1) of the Council Directive 2006/112/UK ('the VAT Directive)?

(2)   Would these services be exempt under Article 135(1) of the VAT Directive?

The ECJ considered that the difference between the purchase price of the cryptocurrency that Mr Hedqvist proposed to purchase and the sale price of this currency would constitute the relevant consideration.[6] The ECJ also considered that there was a direct link between the consideration and the service provided.[7] The ECJ, therefore, held that the exchange of fiat currency for cryptocurrency and vice versa constituted the supply of a service for consideration for the purposes of Article 2(1)(c) of the VAT Directive.[8]

---

[3] Revenue and Customs Brief 9 (2014): Bitcoin and other cryptocurrencies, 3 March 2014, VAT treatment of Bitcoin and similar currencies.

[4] Revenue and Customs Brief 9 (2014): Bitcoin and other cryptocurrencies, 3 March 2014, VAT treatment of Bitcoin and similar currencies.

[5] Case C-264/14, [2016] STC 372.

[6] Ibid, *at* para 29 citing *First National Bank of Chicago*, C-172/96, [1999] QB 570, at paragraph 33, where it was held that where a taxpayer makes a profit on the spread of the purchase and sale of foreign currency this constitutes consideration in the same way as it would have if the taxpayer had charged a commission.

[7] Ibid, at para 30.

[8] Ibid, at para 31.

However, the ECJ also held that the exchange of fiat currency for cryptocurrency and vice versa was exempt from VAT pursuant to Article 135(1)(e) of the VAT Directive. While Article 135(1)(e) of the VAT Directive is expressed to exempt transactions involving 'currency, banknotes and coins used as legal tender', impliedly the ECJ considered that Article 135(1)(e) should extend to virtual currencies where they are used as a means of payment, although this not free from doubt.[9] Whatever the case, HMRC seems happy to accept that where cryptocurrency is used as a form of payment for goods and services, the supply of cryptocurrency itself is an exempt supply,[10] although the goods or services purchased may be subject to VAT in the usual way.

MINING ACTIVITIES AND VERIFICATION

15.3   HMRC consider that income received from Bitcoin/cryptocurrency mining activities are outside the scope of VAT, and therefore not subject to VAT.[11] HMRC consider that this is the case because there is an insufficient link between any economic activity, and the consideration received.

HMRC consider that income received by miners for verification is exempt from VAT pursuant to Article 135(1)(d) of the VAT directive on the basis that they are 'transactions including payments or transfers'.[12] All nodes on the network perform verification of payment transactions and receive a small reward for this. Presumably, these transactions would also be exempt from VAT.

PURCHASE OF CRYPTOASSETS

15.4   The use of sterling or other fiat currency to purchase a crypto asset will be an exempt supply for VAT purposes.[13]

However, the cryptoasset exchanged could potentially be subject to VAT. It will be necessary to consider the nature of the asset and the legal rights that the taxpayer has acquired.

---

[9] Ibid, at paras 49 to 53.

[10] https://www.gov.uk/government/publications/tax-on-cryptoassets/cryptoassets-tax-for-businesses see the VAT section.

[11] Revenue and Customs Brief 9 (2014): Bitcoin and other cryptocurrencies, 3 March 2014, VAT treatment of Bitcoin and similar currencies.

[12] Revenue and Customs Brief 9 (2014): Bitcoin and other cryptocurrencies, 3 March 2014, VAT treatment of Bitcoin and similar currencies.

[13] *VATA 1994, Sch 9, Group 5, item 1.*

A recent notable example is the tokenisation of Andy Warhol's painting '14 electric chairs'.[14] It is not totally clear whether this artwork was situated in the UK. If the painting was situated in the UK, UK VAT would be payable by the seller in the usual way.

CAPITAL RAISING

15.5   If the purpose of the ICO is to raise capital, either debt or equity, it should be neither the supply of a good nor a service and would fall outside the scope of VAT.[15]

UTILITY TOKENS AND VAT

15.6   Over the past couple of years, ICO's have become an increasingly popular way for a founder or entity to fund a project. Many of these ICO's take place on the Ethereum platform. Investors buy tokens, and these tokens give the investor a right to acquire a product or service at a future point in time. These tokens are recorded on Ethereum's blockchain infrastructure. The right to acquire the relevant product or service may be explicitly stated to be conditional, and if so, will often be executed by way of a smart contract on the blockchain. In many cases, the right to acquire the product or service will effectively be conditional on the success of the project itself.

This raises a number of interesting issues as to whether the supply of the good or service will be subject to VAT in the UK:

1   Is the supply made in the UK?
2   If yes, how is the supply characterised?
3   If there a prepayment for the supply?
4   Does the issuance of the token constitute a voucher for VAT purposes to which special rules apply?

Is there a supply of a goods or services in the UK?

Where there is a supply of goods or a supply of services this will be subject to VAT. The VAT Directive guides what amounts to a supply of goods or a supply of services, and this is reflected in the VATA 1994.

---

[14] https://blog.maecenas.co/andy-warhols-14-small-electric-chairs-to-be-sold-in-blockchain-art-auction/.
[15] *Kretztechnik AG v Finanzamt Linz* (Case C-465/03) [2005] All ER (D) 414 (May) paragraph 25 to 27. It should be noted that the rights acquired by an investor in an ICO may be quite opaque.

Article 14(1) of the VAT Directive states that:

'Supply of goods' shall mean the transfer of the right to dispose of tangible property as owner.'

Article 24(1) of the VAT Directive states that:

'Supply of services' shall mean any transaction which does not constitute a supply of goods.'

Clearly, cryptocurrency and cryptoassets are not tangible property and therefore will constitute a supply of services for the purposes of the VAT Directive. The imposition of UK VAT will be obliged to characterise the supply as one of services pursuant to the VAT Directive.

Is yes, how is the supply characterised?

The leading case on how a supply should be characterised is *Card Protection Plan Ltd v Customs and Excise Commissioners*:[16]

1   Where the transaction comprises a bundle of features or acts, regard must be had to all the circumstances in which the transaction took place;[17]
2   Every supply of a service must be regarded as distinct and independent;[18]
3   However, there is a single supply where:
   a   One element constitutes the principal service because it constitutes an aim in itself for a customer, while other elements are ancillary services because they don't constitute an aim in themselves for the customer, but instead support the principal service.[19] The ancillary services will share the tax treatment of the principal service; and
   b   Where two or more elements supplied by a taxable person to the consumer are too closely linked that they objectively form a single indivisible supply, they should be treated as such, rather than being artificially split;[20]
4   It is particularly important to analyse the contractual relationship/documents of the parties in characterising the supply, and to have regard to the context of the transaction, including the economic context, which may alter this and consider the whole of the taxpayer's relationship with its customers to discover the true nature of the supply.[21]

However, where a project is pre-funded, an issue arises as to the precisely when VAT is payable.

---

[16] (Case C-349/96) [1999] STC 270, [1999] ECR I-973.

[17] *Card Protection Plan Ltd v Customs and Excise Commissioners* (Case C-349/96) [1999] All ER(D) 201, at [28].

[18] Ibid, at [29].

[19] *Levob Verzekeginen BV v Staatssecretaris van Financien* (Case C-41/04) [2006] STC 766 at [21].

[20] *Levob Verzekeginen BV v Staatssecretaris van Financien* (Case C-41/04) [2006] STC 766 at [22], *Card Protection Plan Ltd v Customs and Excise Commissioners* (Case C-349/96) [1999] STC 270 at [29].

[21] *Secret Hotels2 Ltd (formerly Med Hotels Ltd) v Revenue and Customs Commissioners* [2014] UKSC 16, [2014] STC 937, [2014] 2 All ER 685 at [31]–[35] referred to in *Findmypast Ltd v Revenue and Customs Commissioners* [2017] CSIH 59. [2017] STC 2335 at [19].

DOES PAYMENT FOR A TOKEN GIVING A RIGHT TO ACQUIRE A PRODUCT OR SERVICE AMOUNT TO 'PREPAYMENT' OF A PRODUCT OR SERVICE?

15.7 Lord Drummond Young observed in *Findmypast Ltd v HMRC*[22] that VAT is generally payable at the time that a good or service is supplied.[23] However, where there is a prepayment for the good or service, or an invoice is issued before payment is made, VAT is due at this earlier time.[24]

The question arises, can a token issued for an ICO constitute the prepayment for a good or service?

There are two cases relevant to an ICO that have considered this issue.

The first was *Findmypast Ltd v Revenue and Customs Commissioners*[25] in which the Scottish Court of Session considered an appeal by the taxpayer from the Upper Tribunal.

The taxpayer ran an online business providing access to ancestry websites that it either owned or have licensed access to. The service could be access by either:

(1) paying for a subscription for a fixed time; or

(2) using the 'Pay As You Go' ('PAYG') system in which credits were purchased that were valid for a fixed time. After expiry, they could be renewed if the customer purchased further credits within two years of expiry.

The taxpayer claimed repayment of the VAT on credits that had expired, on the basis that VAT was due when the credits were redeemed, and the customer downloaded a document or record. HMRC refused the claim contending that a supply for a package of rights and services that conferred the taxpayer the right to search for and download particular documents. In the alternative, HMRC contended that the customer made a prepayment for these services. The taxpayer appealed. The matter ultimately went up to the Scottish Court of Session.

Characterising the service/supply was crucial. Lord Drummond Young, giving judgment for the court, considered that a customer gave consideration and acquired PAYG credits for the ability to view and access documents. The PAYG credits did not in themselves, therefore, constitute a

---

[22] [2017] CSIH 59.
[23] Article 63 of the VAT directive (Directive 2006/112/EC), *VATA 1994, s 1(2)*.
[24] Article 65 of the VAT directive, *VATA 1994, s 6(4)*.
[25] [2017] CSIH 59.

supply. The search facility was available to members of the public in order to entice them to buy credits, and he considered that consideration given by the customer could therefore not extend to this search facility.

In relation to whether there was a prepayment for the services, Lord Justice Drummond held that:

(1) There must be precise identification of the goods or services supplied; and

(2) There must be a direct link between the goods or services supplied and the consideration: reciprocity. This was fundamental;

(3) Characterising the supply in line with the principles outlined above, and in a practical manner was crucial to answering these matters.[26]

In relation to element (2), Judge Drummond Young considered that there was sufficient uncertainty in relation to the transaction that there could not be said to be a direct link between the service to be supplied and the consideration.[27] In particular, it was uncertain:

(1) Whether the chargeable event, the accessing of a document, would ever occur; and

(2) The number of credits to access a document. In the terms and conditions, this could be changed.[28]

Lunar Missions Limited v HMRC[29] is a second very recent case that may potentially be relevant to whether the issue of an ICO constitutes a prepayment for VAT purposes. *Lunar Missions* concerned a taxpayer company that raised funding through the crowd-funding platform 'Kickstarter' to send a spacecraft to the moon to conduct scientific research. Supporters of the project could pledge different amounts of money. Those who pledged £60 were entitled to a 'voucher' that entitled them to digital space in a memory box, or physical space to store a strand of hair, or both. The first-tier tribunal considered that this was a contractually binding obligation on the taxpayer company towards supporters who pledged £60 or more.[30]

The first-tier tribunal followed the principles laid down by the Court of Session in *Findmypast Ltd*. They considered that:

(1) There must be a direct link between the consideration and the goods/services to be supplied (reciprocity); and

(2) Therefore, there must be precise identification of the goods or services to be supplied.[31]

---

[26] *Findmypast Ltd v Revenue and Customs Commissioners* [2017] CSIH 59 Lord Drummond Young at [46] and [47].
[27] Ibid, Lord Drummond Young at [51].
[28] Ibid, Lord Drummond Young at [48].
[29] [2019] UKUT 0298 (TCC).
[30] Lunar Missions Limited v HMRC [2018] UKFTT 007 (TC).
[31] *Lunar Missions Limited v HMRC* [2018] UKFTT 007 (TC) at [59].

The first-tier tribunal observed that the promotional material of *Lunar Missions* recognised that it was uncertain if the mission would launch, and the entire project was inherently uncertain.[32] The first-tier tribunal, therefore, considered that it was uncertain if anything at all would be supplied at the time that the pledge was made and therefore it could not be said there had been a prepayment for the service.[33] These matters were not challenged by HMRC on appeal to the Upper Tribunal.[34]

COULD AN ICO BE CONSIDERED TO BE A SINGLE PURPOSE FACE VALUE VOUCHER?

15.8   Where an ICO is undertaken, and a right is granted for a product or service to be redeemed sometime in the future, it may potentially be a 'face value' voucher.

'Face value voucher' is defined in *VATA 1994, Sch 10A, para 1* as follows:

'(1) In this Schedule 'face-value voucher' means a token, stamp or voucher (whether in physical or electronic form) that represents a right to receive goods or services to the value of an amount stated on it or recorded in it.

(2) References in this Schedule to the 'face-value' of a voucher are to the amount referred to in subparagraph (1) above.'

VATA 1994, Sch 10A, para 2 states that the issue of a 'face value' voucher or the subsequent supply of it, is a supply of services for the purposes of the Act.

VATA 1994, Sch 10A, paras 3 and 4 then disapply the 'face value' voucher rule in the case of 'credit vouchers' and 'retail vouchers'. That is, where a person ultimately undertakes to provide goods or services upon redemption of the voucher.

However, *VATA 1994, Sch 10A, para 7A* then disapplies the rules in *paras 2, 3 and 4* in the case of 'single purpose vouchers'. A 'single purpose voucher' is a 'face value' voucher that represents a right to receive goods or service of one type that are subject to a single rate of VAT. *VATA 1994, Sch 10A, para 7A* effectively removes a 'face value' vouchers that is a 'single purpose' voucher from *Sch 10A*. 'Single purpose' vouchers are subject to VAT are the time of issue.

It should be noted that from 1 January 2019 *Finance Act 2019* has implemented Council Directive (EU) 2016/1065, and there is now only a distinction between 'single purpose'

---

[32] Ibid, at [62].
[33] Ibid, at [62].
[34] 2019 UKUT 0298 (TCC) at [61].

vouchers that are subject to VAT at the time of issue and on each transfer of the voucher, and 'multi-purpose' vouchers that are only subject to VAT are the time of redemption.

It is then crucial to determine whether the issue of a token/ICO is:

(1)   a 'face value' voucher; and

(2)   if it is a 'face value' voucher whether it is 'single purpose' voucher.

Voucher cases are typically fact sensitive and turn on their own facts.

Is a token/ICO a 'face value' voucher?

15.9   Lord Drummond Young in *Findmypast Ltd v Revenue and Customs Commissioners*[35] stated that:

> 'The essence of a face-value voucher is that it is a physical or electronic document that *represents* a right to receive goods or services to a specified amount'.[36]

The background to *Findmypast Ltd* was discussed extensively at 15.7 above. Lord Drummond Young giving judgment on behalf of the Court of Sessions concluded that the PAYG credits/ vouchers that were issued by the taxpayer were:

> 'mere credits allowing a customer to view and download particular documents'; and

> 'they were not purchased for their own sake but as a means to view or download documents'.[37]

Lord Drummond Young further noted that the PAYG credits could be transferred at the point they were issued, but not after that, and in this respect, they were different from 'face-value' vouchers.[38]

For all of the above reasons Lord Drummond Young considered that the PAYG credits/ vouchers, in that case, did not 'represent the right to receive services' but were 'mere credits', and as such, they were not 'face-value vouchers'.[39]

However, this can be contrasted with *Lunar Missions*. The facts of *Lunar Missions* are outlined at **15.7**. Both parties ran their case on the basis that the voucher issued by the taxpayer

---

[35] *Findmypast Ltd v Revenue and Customs Commissioners* [2017] CSIH 59.
[36] Ibid, Lord Drummond Young at [59].
[37] Ibid, Lord Drummond Young at [60].
[38] Ibid, Lord Drummond Young at [60].
[39] Ibid, Lord Drummond Young at [60].

company to a customer, that entitled that customer to digital or physical space on a spacecraft, represented 'the right to receive services'.[40] This is was what ultimately found by the FTT in that case.[41]

Does the voucher 'represent a right to receive goods or services to the value of an amount stated on it'

15.10   Lord Drummond Young giving judgment for the court in *Findmypast Ltd* considered that this requirement was not met. In particular, the value of the PAYG credits/voucher could not be discovered from the voucher itself, but from the accounting system at any particular point in time.[42] Also, he held that the value of the credits could only be determined at the point of redemption.[43]

As such, Lord Drummond Young considered that the further requirements of a 'face value' voucher, that the voucher 'represent a right to receive goods or services *to the value of an amount stated on it*', were not satisfied in *Findmypast Ltd*.

SINGLE PURPOSE VOUCHER?

15.11   In the event that a token/ICO is a 'face value' voucher, it is necessary then to consider whether it is a 'single purpose' voucher within *VATA 1994, Sch 10A, para 7A*. If it is, VAT will be payable by the issuer at the time of issue and at the time of each transfer.

If it is not, prior to 1 January 2019, it is likely to be a 'credit voucher' to which VAT is payable at the time of redemption or a 'retail voucher' to which VAT is payable on transfer or at the time of redemption. After 1 January 2019, it will likely be a 'multi-purpose' voucher to which VAT is payable at the time of redemption.

Lunar Missions is the main authority in relation to ICO's to have considered this matter. The parties, in that case, argued the matter on the basis that they accepted the FTT's conclusion that the issue of the voucher fell within *VATA 1994, Sch 10A, para 7A*.[44] The Upper Tribunal ultimately considered that the taxpayer issuer making a 'single purpose' supply because their

---

[40] *Lunar Missions Limited v HMRC* [2018] UKFTT 007 (TC) at 65.
[41] *Lunar Missions Limited v HMRC* [2018] UKFTT 007 (TC) at 68.
[42] Ibid, Lord Drummond Young at [61].
[43] Ibid, Lord Drummond Young at [62].
[44] Lunar Missions Ltd v HMRC [2019] UKUT 0298 (TCC) at [52].

supply fell squarely in the principles laid down in *Lebara Ltd v Revenue and Customs Commissioners.*[45] Essentially, the issue of the voucher provided the taxpayer with all the necessary information they needed to obtain the supply, and there was effectively a legal relationship between the issuer and the customer by which the issuer received remuneration, and the customer was able to obtain the right to digital of physical space on the spacecraft. As such, there was a supply at that point.[46] While the Upper Tribunal considered that there were uncertainties as to whether the underlying supply would ever be made, they had no doubt that a supply had been made at the time of the issuer of the voucher, and the uncertainty that the underlying supply may never be made was no different from the circumstances on a phone card issuer in *Lebara*.

---

[45] (Case C-520/10) EU:C; 2012;264, [2012] STC 1536.
[46] *Lunar Missions Ltd v HMRC* [2019] UKUT 0298 (TCC) at [69].

Chapter 16

Conclusion

16.1 Cryptocurrency and Blockchain technologies have generated enormous amounts of publicity. The tremendous interest in cryptocurrency driven by Blockchain technologies is that they potentially offer a cheaper, more secure, more efficient alternative to the traditional banking model for processing transactions. These benefits are clearly attractive from a consumer point of view. In theory, this should mean lower transaction costs which should feed through in to lower consumer prices, without sacrificing the integrity of the traditional banking model.

The interest in cryptocurrency and Blockchain technologies that was sparked by, among other things, Ben Bernake's letter to the US Senate Committee on Homeland Security and Government Affairs back in 2013 has spawned numerous starts ups in London and Silicon Valley seeking to utilise these technologies to disrupt the traditional banking model.

Thus far, no one has succeeded in commercialising these technologies on a wide scale in the retail space. Facebook has the best opportunity to take cryptocurrency mainstream, however, they face numerous regulatory hurdles in the United States, the EU and elsewhere in trying to get their project off the ground. It is a matter of speculation as to whether they will be able to do this and to what extent they will succeed if they do.

There is no question that cryptocurrency and Blockchain technologies are here to stay. It is a matter of speculation as to just how big they become and just how fast this technology progresses in revolutionising different industries.

Cryptocurrency has raised numerous novel challenges for both taxpayers and HMRC that have been addressed in this publication. The issue of whether a non-domiciled individual can use the remittance basis for profits subject to capital gains tax realised from the sale of cryptocurrency is one that may well be resolved in the courts.

As cryptocurrency markets develop and potentially go mainstream, they will likely become more sophisticated and more regulated. It may well be that the holder of cryptocurrency has the legal right to sue an entity in the group that issued the cryptocurrency. This may of itself also solve the tax treatment of non-domiciled individuals and whether they can use the remittance basis for capital gains tax purposes.